🞕 Stefan Hunziker

>>> Dedicated to all of those who live the white dream

Published by Mountain Sports Press

Distributed to the book trade by:
PUBLISHERS GROUP WEST

Bill Grout, Editor-in-Chief
Alan Stark, Associate Publisher
Basti Polzelbauer, Art Director, Illustrator (Germany)
Michelle Klammer Schrantz, Art Director
Scott Kronberg, Associate Art Director
Karin Betzler, Layout (Germany)
Jan Christoph Imberi, Illustrator (Germany)
Stefan Österreicher, Translator (Austria)
Chris Salt, Managing Editor
Andy Hawk, Sales Representative

ISBN 0-9724827-3-3

Printed in Canada by Friesens Corporation

Mountain Sports Press
929 Pearl Street, Suite 200
Boulder, CO 80302
303-448-7617

Freeriding and freeskiing are dangerous sports. In high-mountain areas there are
always risks: avalanches, falling rocks, glacier crevasses and more. The authors
believe that backcountry riding and skiing can be done with very low risk. We
wrote this book to help riders and skiers manage their risk of triggering avalanches.
Neither the authors or publisher accept any responsibility for loss or damage
occurring to riders or skiers by using the risk management methods provided
in this book.

powder guide

managing avalanche risk

Tobias Kurzeder   Holger Feist   Patrick Reimann   Peter Oster
Translation by Stefan Österreicher
Published by Mountain Sports Press

>> Preface: A Dream Turned Nightmare

It was a Sunday in January, the worst day of my life. The day one of my best friends was killed in a slab avalanche.

There had been a big dump that weekend, and everyone knows what that means — powder! Thorsten, Andi and I originally wanted to tour the backcountry on snowshoes and snowboards, but then we thought it would be too dangerous due to the high avalanche hazard. So we decided to go to a small ski area in Bregenzerwald, Austria. The area is a bit of a secret. Andi practically grew up there, and Thorsten and I also knew it well. We were all experienced riders. We felt confident that we'd be safe there.

We took Andi's car. There was tons of snow, and it was foggy. When we finally got there, we were in a hurry to get dressed and make first tracks. Before we set off we had a little snack and a sip of schnapps from a hip flask that Thorsten got from his girlfriend. Then we went up the cable car and hit the slopes.

It was fantastic!

Visibility was very poor, but who cared? We had lots of snow and ungroomed trails. Whenever we stopped, we were hip-deep in snow. We did the first few runs together, then I lost my friends; I couldn't keep up with them, but I enjoyed myself anyway.

Then something happened that should have been a warning. Because of poor visibility, I took the wrong trail. I tried to cross a field to get back on the right track. Suddenly I was up to my shoulders in snow, and everything was white. Between the two trails, there was a little valley that had completely filled with powder. It took a lot of time and energy to free myself.

In the afternoon the three of us joined up again. We took a chairlift to the summit for our last ride of the day. My two friends were like kids with a new toy; there was a sparkle in their eyes. Since we hadn't much time left, we decided to go to the other side of the valley.

We rode together to the midway point, where we could take a trail that led to the other side. My two friends had no patience for that, however, and wanted to ride through the forest. Feeling too tired, I refused. We agreed to meet at the base on the other side of the valley. Little did I know that these were to be the last words I would speak with my friends...my God, what a thought!

About 10 minutes later, I was at the base. They didn't show up. After waiting half an hour, I rode down to the valley, hoping to meet them at the parking lot. I thought that perhaps they had taken the cable car for another ride, or maybe they had gotten stuck and had to walk out. Anyway, they were together, so they should have been safe. I imagined so many things, but I had no idea what had really happened.

Time passed, nobody turned up and it snowed and snowed. Expecting them to show up any minute, I stood by the car, freezing, as the parking lot emptied and fewer and fewer skiers and snowboarders came down the trail. I thought that it wouldn't surprise me if they were the last to leave the mountain. About two hours later it got dark, and I got really worried. I asked a lift operator who was about to call it a day whether I should wait another half hour or inform Search & Rescue. He took me to his office and reported the incident to his manager. I described the situation as precisely as I could, and the search began immediately. The rescue team grew in number until about 60 people were involved, but there was no trace of my friends. The head of the SAR team asked me to take him to the spot where we had split up. It felt strange to get back to that place. The search continued throughout the night — without success.

Later on, the operation had to be suspended because conditions had become too dangerous for the rescue team. There was 45 inches of new snow. The following morning the search continued. Somebody discovered Thorsten's goggles, and soon they found Thorsten and Andi. I was told that one of them was alive; the other was dead. They had been buried for 20 hours. My worst nightmare had come true. Together with Thorsten's uncle and sister, who had arrived at the ski area in the meantime, I had to identify Thorsten's body. Andi, his body temperature down to 75 degrees Fahrenheit, was immediately taken to the hospital in Feldkirch. Andi was extremely lucky and survived. Thorsten had died soon after being buried by the avalanche.

They had gotten stuck in a little valley where the slope flattened out. Standing upright, they were buried by eight to 10 feet of snow.

We had thought we'd have a great weekend, just like so many times before. That weekend I had to go back home without my friends. Before I set off, I had to pick up their snowboards at the local police station. For a moment, I thought it was unfair that this had happened to us. It had happened so fast and without warning. I had often heard of avalanche accidents, and often thoughtlessness was the cause, but none of us had ever been directly involved. We never thought that it could happen to us.

On Thursday, the following week, Thorsten was buried. Together with five other friends, I had to carry his coffin.

I wouldn't wish that experience even on my worst enemy.

—Ibo Kilicoglu

⁝ Contents

>> Chapter 5
: What to Do in Case of an Accident— Rescue and First Aid

>> Chapter 6
: Smart Freeriding and Applied Avalanche Safety

>> Chapter 7
: Info: Avalanche Control, The Environment, Snowmobiling, Responsibility

>> Chapter 8
: Freeriding = A Sport for Those Who Use Their Heads

>> Chapter 9 : Resources

>> Introduction

👁 Richard Walch △ St. Moritz, Switzerland ᕯ Holger Feist

Freeriding or freesking in untouched powder snow beyond the crowded trails is one of the most rewarding experiences in life. Anybody who has ever spent a whole day floating through endless powder knows how addictive freeskiing and freeriding can be. But deep inside the snowpack, there is looming danger — the potential for avalanches.

The harmless-looking snowpack is not just a wolf in a sheep's skin, it is more of a tiger in a lamb's skin: unpredictable, treacherous, extremely fast and absolutely deadly.

PowderGuide was written for snowboarders and skiers who want to learn more about avalanches and mountain terrain, whether they are driven by curiosity or by the wish to survive and improve their skills. Good freeriding and freeskiing requires experience, good technique, knowledge and a feeling for snow and mountain terrain. And it takes a lot of time in the backcountry to acquire these skills.

Riding and skiing out-of-bounds involves continuous and independent decision making. Because of the potentially deadly consequences for making a mistake, freeriders and freeskiers need to use their brains.

PowderGuide provides you with the necessary knowledge to independently assess the dangers and opportunities of the mountains. When you move out-of-bounds, you are always exposed to avalanche hazard. It is every freerider's and freeskier's responsibility to deal with the phenomenon of avalanches.

Unfortunately, avalanche danger is not often directly recognizable. Therefore, this book deals with avalanche-related issues such as terrain, snowpack, weather and, of course, boarders and skiers who may trigger slides.

Throughout the book, when we talk about freeriders or freeskiers, we don't differentiate between snowboarders and skiers, because they are all looking for the same thing — plumes of powder, untouched nature and a taste of adventure. When an avalanche happens, there are only victims.

Snow is always cold and white, but it has many different qualities. One day the snowpack is solid and you may surf it without worrying about avalanches. On another day, conditions may have created an unstable snowpack that can make freeriding life threatening after a snowfall of only four inches (10 cm). Freeriding means that you expose yourself, consciously or unconsciously, to a higher risk than when you engage in most other sports. In return you may be rewarded with an unforgettable experience. Those who stay aware of the higher risk and try to manage it have the best chance to experience countless perfect powder runs to come.

PowderGuide provides you with tried and tested methods for independent and responsible avalanche risk management, so that your dream of freeskiing does not turn into a nightmare. This method was developed by the renowned avalanche expert Werner Munter. Large parts of the **PowderGuide** are based on Munter's lifetime achievement — a book published in German under the title *3x3 Lawinen*, which will probably be published in English in the winter of 2004. We thank Werner Munter for his active support. His 3x3 Filter and Reduction Method provides all freeriders and freeskiers with a practical way to make independent avalanche risk assessments in the backcountry.

Since good freeriding and avalanche "snow-how" can be learned only in the mountains, it is vital that you take an avalanche course for implementing the theoretical knowledge acquired by reading this book.

Good powder days are a gift of nature. Snow-how, respect for nature and a little bit of luck allow you to experience unforgettable days in the mountains.

Don't forget to manage your risk. The mountain is always more powerful!

—Tobias Kurzeder, Holger Feist, Patrick Reimann, Peter Oster, Sebastian Pölzelbauer

THE ABC OF LIFE SAVING:

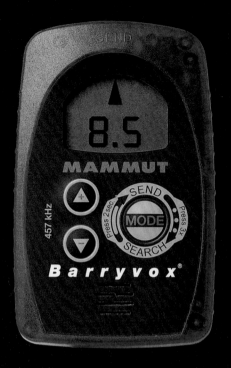

A: SWITCH ON SEARCH MODE
B: FOLLOW DISPLAY INSTRUCTIONS
C: RESCUE

Locating people buried under avalanches is faster and more reliable with MAMMUT Barryvox.
basic functions have been optimized for simple operation. Technical data: small and light [170 g including batteries], approx. 60 m range, can transmit for over 300 hours. Additional functions for professionals.
For further information:
USA: Climb High, phone +1 802 985 50 56, fax +1 802 985 91 41, Email info@climbhigh.com
Canada: Jim Sandford, phone +1 604 892 20 73, fax +1 604 892 20 75, Email sandford@telus.net
www.mammut.ch

>> Chapter 1. The Mountain

☞Richard Walch △ Arlberg, Austria

Mountain Areas and Avalanches

In the winter of 1999, the Alps experienced a catastrophic avalanche cycle. February alone saw more than 1,000 gigantic snow slides. These avalanches caused devastating destruction and claimed numerous lives. Massive snowfalls were accompanied by low temperatures and high winds. These conditions produced avalanches of unprecedented size that destroyed everything that was in their way, including ancient buildings that had been erected over 400 years ago in presumably safe locations. Some of these avalanches had crown fracture lines that exceeded 30 feet (10 meters) in height. Despite dramatic rescue efforts, many victims could not be saved, and entire villages had to be evacuated. The avalanches were so enormous that they cut huge swaths through mountain forests, broke the trees like kindling and reduced them to heaps of debris.

Why should we be concerned with catastrophic events that took place in Europe a few years ago? Because avalanches occur in all snow-covered mountain areas of the world! Humans who settled in Alpine areas generations ago adapted their lifestyles to the dangers of their environments. For a long time these early mountain settlers imagined avalanches (quite understandably) to be demons bringing death from hell.

Catastrophic avalanche.　　ⓒ Swiss Federal Institute for Snow and Avalanche Research, FISAR

Living in this environment day by day and year after year, the mountain people soon came to understand that certain weather and snow conditions increased the danger and caused the snow to slide. They learned to live with the danger and defiantly rebuilt their houses after the houses were destroyed by avalanches.

Unlike in Europe, high alpine regions of North America are only sparsely populated. Just as in other developed countries, the mountains have become important recreation areas that attract visitors seeking a vacation, pursuing outdoor activities or looking for adventure.

In the second half of the 20th century, man started to make alpine environments safer for mountain settlers and visitors and reduce the danger for roads and railways. In Europe, entire mountains were covered in avalanche defense structures, but even the most technically advanced and costly constructions could never completely eliminate risks. The avalanches in Europe in 1999 showed once again that despite all scientific progress, nature is still stronger than any man-made defense structures.

The mountain ranges of North America formed 65 to 100 million years ago, and their development is still not complete. Some areas continue to rise, while others are eroded by ice, snow, water, wind and frost. The gigantic glaciers of the ice ages carved out deep valleys and created large lakes. The mountains that now attract so many skiers and snowboarders are the result of complex processes that have been going on for millions of years. Today these mountains are unique but also highly threatened environments.

Winter recreation is a fairly recent phenomenon that began about a hundred years ago. During the advent of early Alpinism, mountaineers began to venture into areas where — for good reason — no one had deliberately set foot (in winter) before. For a long time, skiing remained an adventure sport and the pursuit of wealthy individuals. It wasn't until the economic upturn following World War II that it developed into a sport for the masses. Large ski resorts were planned and built in North America and Europe. Along with new opportunities for winter recreation, this development exposed visitors to a new, difficult-to-control hazard — avalanches triggered by skiers. Within ski areas, this threat can be largely eliminated by careful monitoring of weather and snow conditions, increased snow compaction by skiers and machines, and the use of explosives to trigger potential snowslides.

For more and more skiers and snowboarders, however, the developed ski area has become too tame, so they now look for adventure out-of-bounds. As a consequence, the number of fatal avalanche accidents has also increased. In the meantime the competition over limited areas of untouched powder has become almost grotesque.

As soon as the gates of ski areas open after control measures are completed, hundreds of powder junkies rush out-of-bounds to draw their lines into the slopes. "The early bird catches the worm" is their motto, and those who want untracked slopes must be fast. Time is often too short for the most elementary safety precautions. At the same time, there is an unprecedented revival of backcountry ski touring. Increasing numbers of skiers and snowboarders are leaving the crowded resorts behind and traveling into the backcountry to look for the peaceful and quiet environment they no longer find (or for the raw, extreme terrain not found) in ski areas, and, of course, for untouched powder slopes.

The enormous technical advances of recent years have led to the development of a whole range of safety equipment — transceivers, avalanche airbag systems and special powder skis, just to mention a few. Despite the use of this modern equipment, it will probably never be possible to completely eliminate all avalanche danger. Many people don't seem to be willing to accept this fact. Many freeriders are tempted to take a higher risk because they rely excessively on their safety equipment (which is actually rescue equipment!). A good system of roads, ski lifts and high-performance snowmobiles make it possible to easily reach extreme terrain in remote high-elevation areas. It is simple to forget that despite of all that progress, the mountains are as dangerous as they have always been. Therefore, all mountain travelers should always observe the following **fundamental rules.**

: Basic Rules for the Backcountry

>>> **Never ride or ski alone!**
If you go solo and have an accident, even if it's just a few hundred yards out-of-bounds, chances are you won't be found until you melt out next spring.

>>> **Don't go freeriding or freeskiing in poor visibility and bad conditions!**
You won't enjoy it anyway, and it is seriously dangerous.

>>> Check the latest **avalanche report** before you set off (see Chapter 3).

>>> Make sure you carry **necessary equipment**. Absolutely indispensable items include:
> **Avalanche transceiver**
> **Avalanche shovel**
> **Avalanche probe**

>>> **For riding or skiing in the backcountry or off-piste** that is invisible from the trails, you also need the following items:
> **First-aid kit**
> **Map, compass, altimeter**
> **Bivouac sack**
> **Food and water**
> **Repair kit**

>>> Since your life and those of your companions depend on your equipment, the basic rule is, **Only the best gear is good enough.**
But **such gear is useless if you don't know how to use it properly.**

> Observe all **warning signs and barriers**. They are there for a reason.

> Even if many ski patrollers still regard freeriders and freeskiers as brainless idiots with suicidal tendencies, try to take their instructions seriously. (After all, they have to rescue and save the lives of skiers and boarders in trouble, sometimes at the risk of their own lives.)

> In critical situations, your life may depend on your companions. Therefore, carefully pick your backcountry partners and think twice about whom to join. The basic rule is, **The best and most experienced rider or skier is responsible for the weaker and less experienced.** Less experienced riders are more at risk, and a perfect day is less enjoyable if you always have to wait for someone.

> Before you ride or ski onto a slope or gully, check out what is above and below you

and consider the dangers they may pose. This is especially true for people below you — don't go before the area is clear, and make sure that no one can be caught in an avalanche that you may trigger.

> Be very careful when riding or skiing onto slopes with sections that are not clearly visible. You should be able to evaluate the entire terrain.

> On steep slopes, always go one at a time.

> When hiking uphill, always keep large distances between group members.

: Slope Angles

Most avalanches occur on slopes of 30 degrees to 45 degrees. In order to assess the avalanche hazard level, it is important to measure or accurately estimate the angle of the slope's steepest section.

Since a few degrees more or less in steepness can decide whether a slope is safe or potentially dangerous, you must be able to estimate a slope's inclination. As long as you are not experienced enough to make reliable estimates, you should use an inclinometer (see Chapter 4).

> As a rule of thumb, slopes steep enough to provide good riding even in deep powder are steeper than 30 degrees and therefore capable of producing avalanches.

Here are more tips for estimating terrain steepness:
> Steep, rocky slopes
> Mounds of debris (moraines) produced by glaciers
> Slopes that produce loose-snow avalanches
  are typically steeper than 39° and therefore classical avalanche terrain

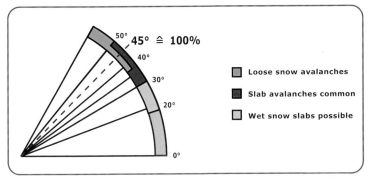

The inclination of a slope is expressed in degrees. A slope angle of 45° corresponds to a gradient of 100%.

: Slope Orientation (Aspect)

Riding and skiing conditions depend on slope orientation, steepness and terrain features. A slope's orientation or aspect is the compass direction the slope faces looking straight down its fall line. Snow conditions are greatly influenced by a slope's orientation to the sun and winds, e.g., whether it is facing south or north, and whether a slope is windward or leeward (downwind). In extreme cases, you may find perfect powder on a north-facing slope and a nasty, icy crust on a south-facing slope that received more solar radiation in the daytime, causing the snowpack to melt and refreeze during the night. Therefore it is important to consider how exposed a slope is to the sun, that is, whether the snow is still loose and powdery or already sticky or whether a melt-freeze crust formed over night has already softened. A south-facing slope receives the strongest direct radiation from the sun at noon. If you are standing on a north-facing slope at midday, the sun is behind you. An east-facing slope receives direct radiation in the morning and a west-facing slope in the afternoon.

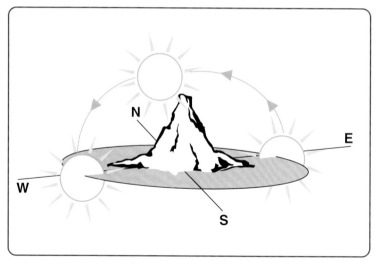

A slope's orientation or aspect is the compass direction looking straight down its fall line. East-facing slopes receive strongest direct radiation in the morning. Around noon, when the sun reaches its highest point, solar warming is at its peak and south-facing slopes receive the most solar radiation. From the afternoon until sunset, radiation is strongest on west-facing slopes.

A compass can be used to determine the exact orientation of a slope. Another method is to use an analog watch. Simply point the hour hand at the sun, then draw an imaginary line between it and the 12 o'clock mark. This line points due south.

In midwinter, the sun moves low across the horizon, therefore inclined surfaces receive more radiation that flat areas. Consequently, a steep (40-degree) south-facing slope receives as much radiation in one day as an east-southeast slope might in two days, an east-facing slope in three days and an east-northeast slope in seven days. A steep north-facing slope is not exposed to a single ray of sunlight between November and January. While the sun is moving so low across the horizon, even small terrain features can have a strong influence on snow conditions. These effects increase in northern latitudes.

From early winter until midwinter, when the sun is moving very low across the horizon, even small terrain features can have a strong influence on snow conditions — each little rock and tree is casting a shadow.

: Slope Shape and Terrain Features

Every freerider and freeskier should be familiar with the following terrain features and their peculiarities.

Gaps in Ridges

Notches and cols in mountain ridges increase wind speed and wind loading.

Large amounts of snow are deposited on the lee (downwind) side.

Ridges and Crests

On the leeward side of ridges, windblown snow can quickly form into thick unstable slabs. Winds also create cornices that sometimes overhang the ridge with many tons of snow. Cornices form when windblown snow decelerates and deposits downwind of a ridge.

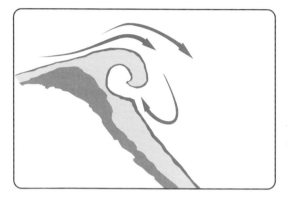

The flatter and wider the ridge, the more snow is deposited on the leeward side.

Many slopes are lined with a **series of ridges**. The snowpack on these ridges is often very shallow; sometimes bare rocks are visible. The gullies between the ridges fill with dangerous slabs of windblown snow, particularly on the lee side. The gullies' flanks are even steeper than the actual gullies.

Gullies and chutes, therefore, pose an increased **avalanche hazard**.

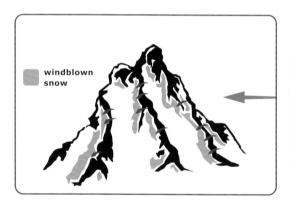

windblown snow

Cross-loading deposits snow in gullies on the lee side of ridges. These cross-loaded gullies are extremely prone to avalanching. Gullies are avalanche paths! Great as the temptation may be, be very careful in chutes and gullies, and below ridges. Ride the ridges, if possible. Windblown snow is also deposited in gullies and behind large terrain features.

V-shaped gullies and creek bottoms can become deadly traps. When an avalanche releases above, they fill up with large amounts of snow so that even a "small" slide can bury a person several yards (meters) deep. Depressions and little bowls at the end of a slope are particularly dangerous traps. Even the flat bottoms of steep slopes are terrain traps. If a rider triggers an avalanche, there is no escape.

Avoid terrain traps, or leave them as quickly as possible!

Steep, open slopes without significant terrain features offer little anchoring for the snow cover. There is no safe place to be. These slopes can produce very large avalanches, must always be approached with extreme caution and can only be considered reasonably safe under very stable conditions.

The typical slope is rounded at the top (convex), subjecting the snow cover to tensile stresses. Compression occurs at the flat (concave) bottom of a slope where the snow supports the snowpack above. If this support is disturbed, an avalanche can be triggered far above.

Steep open slopes always require extreme caution.   ☏Bavarian Avalanche Warning Service

Complex Terrain offers a series of features such as drops, benches, cornices and chutes, and is ideal for freeriding and freeskiing due the variety it offers. Remember that slope orientation and angle can vary greatly within a very small given area. Similar to a minefield, dangerous and safe sections can be found side by side.

Complex or broken terrain often gives an illusion of safety, as the steep areas are broken up by sections of less-steep or even flat areas. However, large avalanches may also sweep through complex terrain. Its depressions and small valleys can then become deadly terrain traps that can bury a rider under large masses of snow.

Glaciers are slow-flowing masses of ice. Their movement and the pressure from their weight create crevasses. Some crevasses can reach a depth of hundreds of feet or several hundred meters! In winter they are often covered by a thin layer of snow that may collapse under the weight of a person. Crevasses have claimed the lives of many mountaineers. Crossing a glacier without a competent guide who knows the area is extremely dangerous. Since glacial ice is moving, crevasses frequently change position.

Know your line!

Richard Walch △ Arlberg, Austria Tommy Brunner

>>Chapter 2: Snow and Avalanches

Powder avalanche. ☎Bavarian Avalanche Warning Service

Snow is more than frozen water

In order to better understand the phenomenon of avalanches we must understand some fundamental things about our favorite element: snow. Snowfall occurs when moist air is cooled in the atmosphere far below 32 degrees Fahrenheit (0 degrees Celsius), forming tiny ice crystals. Depending on conditions during their formation, there are more than 6,000 types of distinct crystals. However, all of them follow a basic hexagonal (six-sided) pattern. Snowflakes form when individual crystals form conglomerates. At temperatures around the freezing point, large snowflakes are falling, while at extremely low temperatures, snow falls as single crystals.

⁞ Types of Snow

> **Powder snow** is the dream of all powderhounds. It falls in the absence of wind and at low temperatures as very small flakes. It contains more than 90 percent air and is therefore light and loose. In fact, it is so dry and **cohesionless** that you won't be able to press it into a snowball. True powder snow creates relatively harmless **loose-snow avalanches**, or **point releases**. However, in terrain traps, point releases can be dangerous and even turn deadly.

When snow is deposited while the wind is blowing, as is usually the case in the mountains, it loses its fluffy consistency and becomes cohesive. **Cohesive new snow** can become a deadly trap when it forms **slab avalanches**. The cohesion may be minimal: Slab avalanches often release on great powder slopes.

Slab avalanche started to slide on top of a weak layer. The deposition zone contains large chunks of snow.   ⊕Thorsten Indra △ Colorado

If snow falls at relatively high temperatures, it forms large and heavy flakes that contain a lot of water. This **moist, new snow** can form **wet loose-snow avalanches** or **wet slab avalanches** on steep slopes. Unfortunately, this sticky snow is more suitable for making snowballs than for skiing or snowboarding.

The avalanche danger soars during a storm when warming temperatures cause heavy, moist snow to fall on the cold and dry snow from earlier in the storm.

> **Graupel** forms when ice crystals collide with supercooled water droplets in the air. The droplets instantly freeze to the crystals and form tiny balls. Graupel is also known as **pellet snow** and can become a dangerous weak layer within the snowpack.

> **Hoarfrost**. Some types of snow crystals do not fall from the sky, but form either on the snow surface as **surface hoar** or on the surface of objects as **rime**.

Surface hoar is the frozen equivalent of summer's dew. Surface hoar grows under clear and calm conditions and at night when moisture from the air condenses on the cold snow surface and forms feathery ice crystals. These crisp, brittle crystals can reach a fairly large size.

Surface hoar: Feather-like crystals glitter on the snow surface. This beautiful decoration can become a deadly weak layer when buried in new snow.
⊕Tyrolean Avalanche Warning Service.

When surface hoar is covered by subsequent layers of new snow, it provides a perfect **weak layer (gliding surface)** for a snow slab. These very thin layers of surface hoar can persist for weeks and are responsible for many avalanche accidents. This is particularly true in the trees, where surface hoar is protected from the wind and sun and becomes buried more often.

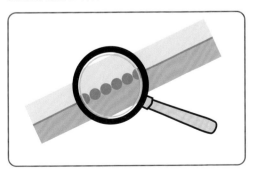

Buried layer of surface hoar — a perfect gliding surface for a snow slab.

> **Rime** forms in foggy and windy conditions on the cold surface of objects. Rime is a good wind indicator, as it always grows into the wind.

Rime grows into the wind.
The wind blew from the right side.

⌦Thorsten Indra △ Lebanon

> **Rain.** From time to time rain falls even in high mountain regions during winter. Rain causes the freeskier's mood to drop, since it causes avalanche hazard to rise drastically and quickly, especially when rain falls on recent new snow. In these conditions, wet-snow avalanches may be triggered. When the entire snowpack starts to slide, exposing the dirt, rocks or grass beneath (avalanches actually love to slide on grass), they are called ground avalanches.

Avalanche danger increases rapidly and dramatically when strong snowfall turns to rain.

A huge ground avalanche.   ⌦Bavarian Avalanche Warning Service.

: The Snowpack

Snow that falls during winter is deposited on the ground in layers of various thicknesses. These layers are composed of different types of snow. Since snow crystals are very fragile and unstable, they constantly change their shape and properties from the instant they form in the atmosphere until the moment they melt on the ground. This process is called **metamorphism**.

Metamorphism plays an important role in avalanche formation. Because of this, freeriders should be familiar with the following four types of metamorphism:

> **Metamorphosis through wind and pressure**
> **Rounding**
> **Faceting**
> **Melt-freeze metamorphism**

☞Bavarian Avalanche Warning Service

A backlighted cross section of a snowpack. The many different layers reflect changing meteorological conditions throughout the winter. Strong snowfalls form thick and even layers, while warm weather and rain create layers of very hard snow or ice.

: Metamorphosis Through Wind and Pressure

Before our powder snow even touches the ground, it may already undergo changes. Wind breaks up the delicate crystals, transports the fragments on the ground and compacts the snow when it is deposited as **windblown snow**. Even though this type of snow may look fairly similar to powder, it reacts differently to stresses. Windblown snow can be soft or tabletop hard, but in either condition it is a slab. Under too much pressure, it easily fractures like a pane of glass and starts sliding as a whole.

Heavily wind-loaded windward slope.   ⚏Bavarian Avalanche Warning Service.

Even in good weather, wind action can deposit large amounts of snow on lee (downwind) slopes. Snow plumes on ridges and around peaks are good indicators of heavy wind loading. True powder snow falls apart if you pick it up in a shovel and shake it lightly. Cohesive windblown snow can be recognized by sharp tracks left behind by skiers or snowboarders. Sometimes each ski leaves a clearly visible, separate track in this type of snow.

> **Fresh deposits of windblown snow are capable of releasing as slab avalanches.**
> **Always avoid recently wind-loaded slopes! They are potential death traps.**

Some people seem to be attracted by dangerous situations. This curious rider walked out too far on an overhanging cornice. With a thumping noise, the cornice broke off and the rider disappeared. He was very lucky and escaped with no more than a scare. Avalanche hazard not only exists in high mountain areas but anywhere where there is snow on steep slopes. This accident occurred at an elevation of only 4,600 ft (1,400 m).

☎Basti Pölzelbauer △ Black Forest, Germany 🏂 Baschi Bender

Rounding: From Stars to Grains

As soon as new snow reaches the ground, it begins to change shape. Depending upon conditions, the new snow crystals may shrink in size and gain strength.

When the snowcover is deep and temperatures relatively warm, the new snow undergoes a process called **rounding**. Rounding leads to settlement and compaction of the snowcover. (The snow crystals sinter.) The process of rounding breaks down the complicated star-like structure of snow crystals. The fine crystal branches shrink as water vapor moves from the extremities to the body of the crystals. The hexagonal stars loose their shape and become smaller, more-rounded grains. Where the grains touch the migrating water vapor forms bonds linking the grains together. At the same time, the content of air in the snowpack is significantly reduced. The tiny grains are closely packed which leads to the settling and compaction of the snowcover. At low temperatures this process is slowed down, while at higher temperatures it occurs faster. The conclusion to draw for freeskiers is that mild weather stabilizes the snowpack quickly and reduces avalanche hazard, while constantly low temperatures keep the avalanche danger high.

Rounding is more prevalent in coastal snowpacks with lots of snow and relatively mild temperatures.

The end products of rounding are strong rounded snow grains. This would mean that we could ski all slopes without worrying about avalanches — if there weren't weak layers, which are often caused by another metamorphic process.

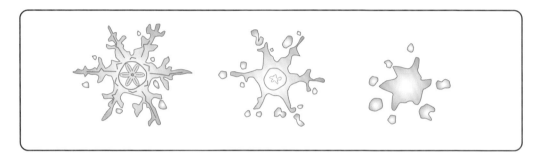

Rounding: Stellar crystals are transformed into granular snow. This process leads to settling and consolidation of the snowpack. The rate of rounding largely depends on temperature.

Faceting: From Stars to Cup-Shaped Grains

When the snowcover is shallow and temperatures cold, the snow loses strength as the snow crystals grow into large and loose grains. Low temperatures at the snow surface and warmer temperatures on the ground underneath create a temperature gradient within the snowpack. The reason for this phenomenon is that the ground rarely freezes, while temperatures on the snow surface continue to fall during cold nights. Just like deep down in a mine, temperatures rise within the snowcover the deeper you go. The shallower the snow, the steeper the temperature gradient. When this temperature gradient is large or strong enough, the snow on the ground begins to sublimate. Water vapor rises and refreezes on the colder snow grains above. The grains do not bond; rather they grow larger with straight sides and sharp angles. Sometimes called sugar snow, the grains become loose and cohesionless, and if the grains continue to grow, facets develop and the grains become cup shaped. This process is also called temperature gradient metamorphism, or faceting, and leads to the formation of depth hoar or fully advanced faceted grains. Faceted snow is a serious weak layer that contributes to longtime and persistent instability. Depth hoar is more common near the ground, but faceted grains can form near the snow surface. During prolonged cold and dry periods, a large temperature gradient can turn the top four to eight inches (10 to 20 cm) of snow into loose, faceted snow. This can improve riding conditions. Once buried by additional snow, it becomes another weak layer in the snowpack. Faceting can also lead to the formation of cavities in the bottom of the snowpack, around large rocks and bushes, and at the edges of gullies.

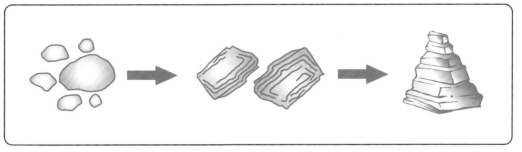

Faceting: As snow grains on the ground sublimate, water vapor refreezes on colder grains above. New cup-shaped crystals grow and sometimes reach a size of half an inch or more (10-20 mm). Formation of depth hoar drastically reduces the snowpack's stability. If new snow is deposited on a foundation of faceted snow, the avalanche danger level remains high for a long time.

Faceting occurs at a very fast rate in shallow snowcovers in the presence of large differences between the temperature of the ground surface and that of the snow surface, and between the temperature of rocks or trees and that of the surrounding snow. Large temperature gradients are common in the early winter and during prolonged dry spells. (Conversely, a weak temperature gradient leads to rounding.) The end product of faceting is large, loose cup-shaped grains that result in a weak layer and unstable layer of snow. The conclusion for freeskiers is that shallow snow and cold temperatures weaken the snowpack. This increases the avalanche hazard during and after the next snowfall. Isolated rocks, bushes and trees promote faceting and create weak spots in the snowpack.

> Shallow snowcovers in early and mid winter (November to January) are particularly dangerous, because faceting is causing the snowpack to lose strength and form fragile depth hoar. The situation gets worse if the weather is sunny and temperatures are low. Faceting occurs frequently in the shallow and cold continental snowpacks of the Rockies and interior ranges.

This avalanche was triggered by skiers in a heavily wind-loaded slope.

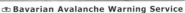

ⓒ Bavarian Avalanche Warning Service

> **Winters with heavy snowfall and areas that generally receive high amounts of snow are less dangerous for freeriders than dry winters and regions with shallow snowpacks.**

Faceting explains why dry winters claim more lives among freeskiers and freeriders than winters with heavy snowfall. Generally, snow conditions vary considerably from region to region, and some areas are characterized by climatic conditions that favor the formation of depth hoar. Areas that usually receive heavy snowfalls (the Coast Ranges of North America and the north slope of the European Alps) and coastal mountain areas are characterized by a deep, homogenous snowcover and direct-action avalanches. Such avalanches occur during or right after storms, and then the situation tends to settle down quickly.

In continental areas with scarce snowfall the situation is entirely different. These regions (the Eastern alpine zone of North America, the Canadian and Colorado Rockies and the Central European Alps) are characterized by more shallow and unstable snowpacks that contain numerous weak layers and may be compared to a pile of pancakes with syrup in between. An avalanche hazard often persists for a longer time in those conditions.

: Melt-Freeze Metamorphism

Everybody gets a little sad when the snow begins to melt.

Now water rules the snowpack. At a temperature of 32 degrees Fahrenheit (0 degrees Celsius), the snow begins to melt and disappear. Snow grains become rounder and settling increases. If this thawing process continues, water content rises to a level that cannot be retained in the snowpack and meltwater percolates to deeper layers. The snow surface now appears undulated and uneven. The high water content and melting between individual grains turns the snow into soft and soggy slush.

If meltwater collects on an impervious layer below or within the snowpack (such as the ground or an ice crust), it may form a lubricating layer that provides a potential sliding surface for an avalanche.

Meltwater collecting on the ground surface or on an ice crust creates a potential gliding surface for an avalanche. A wet snowpack is a warning sign!

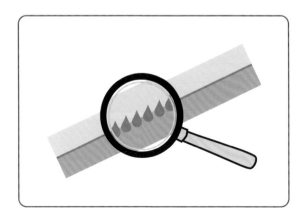

☐ Thorsten Indra △ Lebanon

Late winter or early spring in Lebanon. Ridges are almost bare, while channels and depressions retain considerable amounts of snow.

When snow melted during melt-freeze metamorphosis refreezes on cold nights, it forms a **melt-freeze crust**. When this refrozen top layer softens during the day, it turns into spring snow that provides excellent freeskiing. Repeated cycles of melt and freeze over several days lead to the development of **corn snow**, a favorite surface for riders and skiers. Further melting and increased water saturation softens the entire snowcover and transforms spring snow into **rotten snow** that has no strength. This is a sign of generally high avalanche hazard!

This cycle of thawing and refreezing is typical of spring conditions. However, melt-freeze metamorphism may occur at any time of the year. Even in midwinter, warm winds (a Chinook or foehn), rain or intense solar radiation on a south-facing slope may cause melt-freeze metamorphism.

Thawing increases avalanche hazard in the short term, while subsequent refreezing solidifies and strengthens the snowpack. Plan to start ascents early in the day, when the snow is cold and frozen. Time the descent to start shortly after the snow surface has started to melt and soften. In high altitudes, particularly on glaciers, this cycle may continue over very long periods of time. When spring snow is older than one year, it is called **firn snow**.

: Types of Avalanches

Avalanches are classified according to their manner of starting, form of movement, position of the sliding surface and material deposited in the runout zone. Freeriders should be able to distinguish two basic types of avalanches: **loose-snow avalanches** and **slab avalanches**.

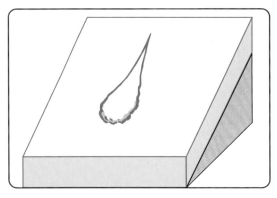

Loose-snow avalanches generally release on very steep slopes (greater than 39 degrees). A basic precondition for the formation of loose-snow avalanches is cohesionless snow (true powder snow or new or old wet snow). This type of avalanche starts from a point, hence the name point release, and then gradually increases speed and width. Point releases can easily be recognized by their characteristic inverted V shape.

Slab avalanches are responsible for most avalanche accidents. Slab avalanches occur when an area of cohesive snow begins to slide on a weak layer. Slab avalanches move very fast and start from a usually well-defined fracture line.

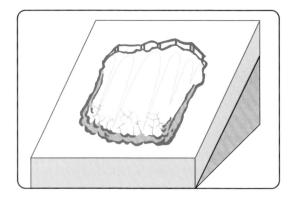

: Loose-Snow Avalanches (or Point Releases)

Loose-snow avalanches often release during or shortly after storms on very steep slopes generally steeper than 39 degrees. Wet loose-snow avalanches also occur in springtime on slopes that receive strong solar radiation leading to moist or wet snow conditions, and with wet new snow or rain.

Loose-snow avalanches start from a point and increase their width and speed as they move along. Their path often takes the shape of an inverted V or a pear. The basic ingredients for a loose-snow avalanche are poor bonding of the top snow layer and low internal cohesion. Movement usually starts in the top layers of the snowpack, and the amount of snow carried by loose snow avalanches is rarely large. Point releases are generally less dangerous for freeriders than slab avalanches. However, a loose-snow avalanche can sweep you off a cliff and give you some unpleasant airtime or bury you in a narrow ravine. Remember that there is no such thing as a harmless avalanche. Even the smallest slide can be deadly.

Loose-snow avalanches in a steep slope exposed to strong solar radiation with wet snowpack. Point releases may also trigger snow slabs (as in this case).

⊕Bavarian Avalanche Warning Service

: Slab Avalanches

Slab avalanches are the main hazard for freeskiers and responsible for the vast majority of fatal avalanche accidents. Dry-snow slabs release in slopes with an inclination of 30 degrees or more. Unfortunately, slope angles between 30 degrees and 50 degrees not only provide the best skiing conditions but also pose the highest avalanche risk. Slopes steeper than 50 degrees are also capable of producing slides. While these steep-slope slides are usually much more shallow than slab avalanches occurring on flatter slopes, they are just as dangerous. In very steep terrain, even a small slide can be very fast and powerful and sweep you off a cliff or down the slope. Wet-snow slabs can release even on shallow slopes.

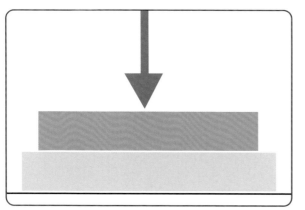

These bricks are subject to the same stresses that snow layers experience in the snowpack. On level ground, their stability depends on their hardness (their resistance to pressure).

 On a slope, the situation changes. Stability now depends on bonding between layers, also called shear strength.

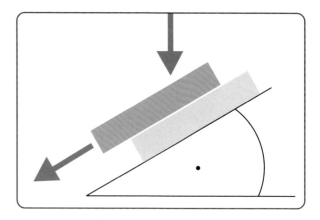

Unfortunately it is very difficult and sometimes impossible to recognize and avoid snow slabs. Slab avalanches are extremely dangerous and hard to predict. Therefore every freerider should know how slabs form, how they release and how they can be avoided. Ninety-five percent of all fatal avalanches are triggered by their victims (or by someone in their group). That's why it is vital to recognize the danger early, that is, before the slab is released. Unlike loose-snow avalanches, slabs reach their full force and speed shortly after they are released. Snow slabs are like booby traps. The moment they are triggered, they strike with full speed and force. Slab avalanches usually have a well-defined fracture line where the slab separates from the rest of the snowpack before it breaks up into smaller blocks as it slides downhill.

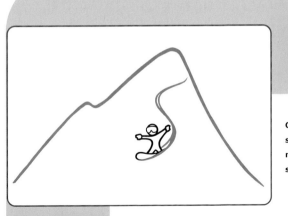

Our little powder junkie has found himself a perfect slope. Wrapped up in excitement over the ride, he's not even thinking about avalanche hazard. Why should he?

He doesn't notice the hollow whumpfing noise of the collapsing snow slab. Cracks are shooting through the snowpack; the slab has been triggered.

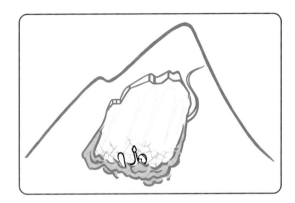

The slab breaks up into large chunks and rushes down the hill at full speed. The dream has turned into a nightmare.

Avalanches may cause catastrophic accidents claiming numerous lives and destroying property and roads. Most of the large avalanches that killed more than 100 people throughout Europe in the winter of 1998–99 were large **powder avalanches**, also known by their German name **staublawinen**. These are huge, destructive powder clouds of snow. Powder avalanches may originate either as loose-snow avalanches or as slab avalanches. When the path is long and steep enough, some of the dry snow may become airborne and turn into an aerosol of fine, diffused snow that moves at speeds of up to 250 miles (400 km) per hour. Behind and under the powder cloud is a mass of flowing snow tumbling and bouncing down the slope. The air blast of powder snow can be as destructive as the flowing snow behind it. Chances of surviving powder avalanches are slim, as the snow dust can be forced into the victim's lungs causing suffocation.

These avalanches descend with such tremendous force that once they have reached the valley floor they may even travel up the opposite side of the valley. Therefore, there are no true islands of safety in the case of staublawinen. Large powder avalanches usually release after extremely heavy snowfall.

A huge powder avalanche in Austria.

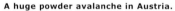

Another type of avalanche that may also cause massive destruction is the wet ground avalanche, or **grundlawine**. Ground avalanches release in warm weather conditions and move along more or less known avalanche paths. They rarely claim lives, as they are fairly slow and predictable, which allows preventive measures such as closing down roads. On the other hand, ground avalanches clean off the snow right down to the ground and include masses of rock, soil, trees and other material. This is why this type of avalanche generally deposits larger masses of debris (deposition zone) than does any other type of slide. Pressure exerted by this heavy material often exceeds 100 tons per square yard (meter).

An avalanche causing catastrophic destruction can not always be classified according to one of the clearly defined groups and may represent a mixed form of different types of avalanches. As ski areas and roads usually remain closed during danger of catastrophic events, it is not absolutely necessary for freeskiers to know detailed definitions of the various types of these potentially large and destructive avalanches.

It is important to understand that anybody who travels outside of controlled ski areas is always exposed to the dangers of mountain environments. Avalanche control measures are limited to clearly defined areas. Out-of-bounds and in the backcountry, there is always a potential avalanche hazard. Fortunately, avalanches usually only release under certain conditions and in certain spots. Freeriders should know how slab avalanches form, how they are triggered and how they can be avoided. This basic knowledge is a precondition for proper risk assessment.

A building destroyed by a powder avalanche.

⊡Tyrolean Avalanche Warning Service △ Tyrol, Austria

⊡

: Wind: The Architect of Snow Slabs

During a storm, new snow is distributed unevenly, creating areas of instability in which the newly formed slab is unable to support its own weight. The snow's weight causes stresses that exceed static friction between individual snow layers, causing slabs to release naturally and slide downhill. However, those spots often retain sufficient support at the top, bottom or at their flanks to remain suspended like a trap, waiting to catch an unwary skier. An untouched slope can be compared to a patchwork quilt. Stable areas and weak spots (hot-spots) can be found close together.

Wind will deposit snow in areas where the wind slows down. That's often on the lee (downwind) sides of ridges and below cols, notches and passes. It also happens, but less obviously, in drop-offs below plateaus and on the downhill side of rolls. Wind also cross-loads slopes parallel to the contour lines. The depositions are then behind the ridges that border gullies.

stable areas

medium

hot-spots

A sloping snowpack is composed of areas with varying stability. Unfortunately it is impossible to identify all unstable spots. Consequently, it is impossible to eliminate all risk.

The snowcover is characterized by its irregular structure.

Terrain features and wind cause very uneven snow deposition.　⌾Richard Walch

In order to assess the avalanche hazard level, you need to know more about stresses and processes occurring in a sloping snowpack. Rounding and melt-freeze metamorphism cause the snow grains to settle and sinter, which means the snow grains get closer together (undergo compaction) and build strong bonds to the other grains around them. Additionally, there is a slow downhill movement called **creep**. The snowpack's individual layers move at different velocities, like different viscosities of oil. Highest rates of creep occur in the top layers. With increasing depth, ground roughness and friction reduce creep. The variation in creep velocities creates shear stresses between individual snow layers.

Shear stresses occurring in a snowpack are opposed by **static friction** between snow layers.

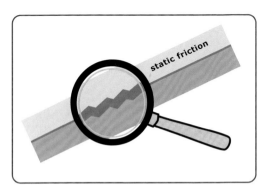

Static friction is the force that holds individual snow layers together. It offers resistance to the stresses that trigger an avalanche.

The distribution of stresses on a slope from top to bottom. Apart from shear stresses, creep also produces tensile stresses in the convex section at the top of the slope and compression stresses at its concave bottom. In these areas the snowpack is particularly sensitive to extra loads.

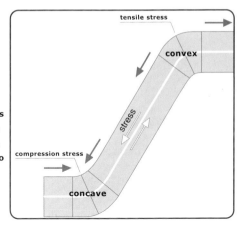

Distribution of stresses varies greatly in a given slope. Overall stability depends on the relationship between snow strength and shear stresses in individual slope sections.

> A slope section is stable if strength exceeds stresses.
> A slope section is unstable (or in a state of critical balance) if stresses almost equal strength.
> A slope section is like a bomb that only needs a spark to explode if stresses exceed strength.
> A weak layer — such as depth hoar, buried surface hoar, ice or crust — reduces friction by creating a weak interface between two layers that can provide the sliding surface for an avalanche. Unfortunately, almost every snowpack contains potential sliding layers.

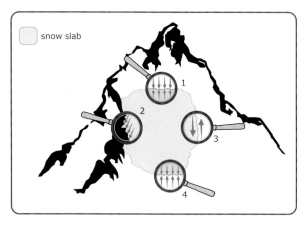

snow slab

A snow slab can hang in a slope like a set trap waiting to be released even though shear strength at its base is lower than shear stress. In this case, shear strength may not be sufficient to prevent a release but the slab is kept in a state of critical balance by one or more of the following forces:

1. Tensile strength (at the top)
2. Lateral shear strength and anchoring around rocks
3. Lateral shear strength at areas with stable snow
4. Compression strength = support at the foot of the slope (bottom)

Slab avalanche occurs when an area of relatively firm, cohesive snow begins to slide on a weak layer, e.g., windblown powder on top of buried surface hoar.

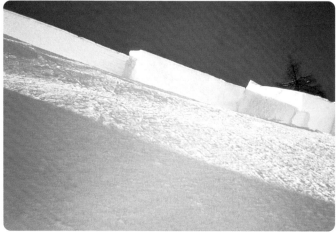

A crown fracture line of a huge slab.

⏺ Bavarian Avalanche Warning Service

Stable slope sections can absorb excess tension from weak spots. However, if the additional load of a skier or new snow increases stress, an **initial failure** may occur in a weak spot and rapidly propagate in all directions until the weak layer fractures throughout the slab, causing the slab to slide. Slabs often release so fast that there is no escape. The initial fracture sometimes occurs at a considerable distance. Remote release is often caused by groups of riders or by vehicles used for grooming. When **avalanche hazard level is high or considerable**, a single rider can cause a fracture at the bottom of an unstable slope. Sometimes you may be able to hear a hollow **whumpf** sound caused by collapsing weak snow layers. Whumpfing noises indicate a life-threatening situation and can be compared with the clicking sound of a cocked gun. The fracture propagates invisibly and at the speed of sound within the snowpack, until it probably releases a large slab on a steep slope.

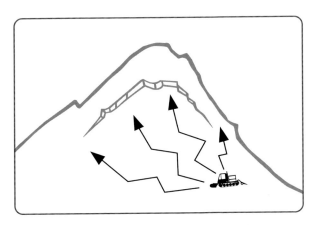

Remote release of a slab avalanche caused by a vehicle. Remote release occurs occasionally whenever avalanche danger is rated Considerable and frequently whenever it is rated High, when the weight of a single rider may suffice to cause initial fracture.

Sometimes, several minor and relatively harmless weak spots interconnect before the slab avalanche is triggered. Consider the following scenario: a group of freeriders visit a suspect avalanche slope. Hidden weak spots (sometimes called superweak zones or hot-spots) lurk like buried mines in a field. The first two riders (or maybe even five or six riders) descend without problems. Maybe the next rider (or seventh or even 10th rider) starts down and crosses a hidden weak spot. The snow grains start to fail due to the additional stress of the rider. If the weak spot is isolated and the snow relatively strong, the stresses are quickly redistributed and the snow stays in place. However, if two or more of these weak spots are close together, the extra stress caused by the rider overwhelms one weak spot, which leads to the failure in another nearby weak spot. Like a line of tumbling dominos, the weak spots start to fail and within a second or two, the slab tears loose. The stiffer and harder the slab, the farther the fracture can propagate and the bigger the avalanche.

When snow conditions are marginally stable and certainly when conditions are unstable, tracks on a slope can lead to a dangerous trap. Say the group of freeskiers and riders in the example above all descend without incident. Spirits are high and so is their confidence that the slope is stable, so they return to the top for a second run. Is the snow stable or have they just not yet hit the right weak spot? Unaware of the trap they have set with their previous run, they dive onto the slope. Maybe it's on this second pass they trigger the avalanche.

The lesson to be learned is that tracks are no safe indication of a slope's stability.

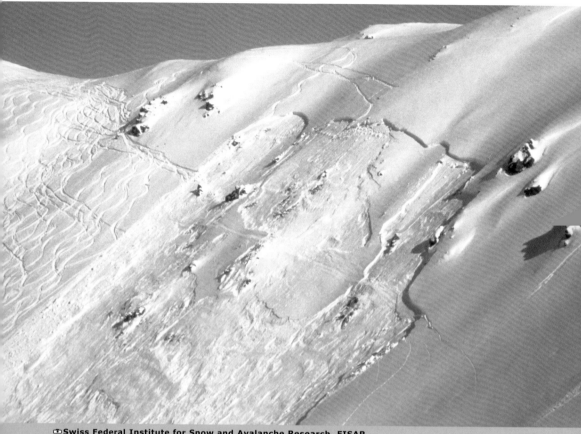

⊡Swiss Federal Institute for Snow and Avalanche Research, FISAR
A slab avalanche on a popular freeride slope. In search of untouched powder, riders venture farther and
farther into steep, rocky terrain until they hit a weak spot.

The steeper the run, the better the fun — and the easier it is to trigger a slab avalanche.

Swiss avalanche researcher Bruno Salm discovered that the amount of stress that
causes a fracture in the snowpack is variable and depends on the speed at which the
stress is applied. Just like honey, snow is able to flow slowly like a very dense liquid and
absorb high stresses if they are applied slowly. Fractures will occur only when stresses
exceed the **critical speed of deformation**. If you have ever tried to run through deep powder
snow, you know that unless you move slowly and shift your weight carefully, step by
step, you will sink deeply into the snow and waste a lot of energy. When a load such as
the weight of your body is applied suddenly — for example, if you jump off a cornice onto
the slope below — stability may be reduced to as little as one 10th of its original value.

Be particularly careful when the avalanche danger level is rated Considerable (or
higher) or when you feel instinctively uncomfortable. If you are not extra cautious, you
may run right into a trap.

Unlike our pile of bricks, the snow is able to deform and absorb stress, but it requires
a lot of time to do so. Even large areas of wind-deposited snow may settle sufficiently to
absorb the stresses applied by a skier. When in doubt, wait. Time and stability are
generally on the side of the patient freeskier.

☜Bavarian Avalanche Warning Service

Snow is deformable. Ten foot (three meter) high fold in gliding moist snow.

Weather and Avalanche Hazard

The avalanche danger level is intimately related to meteorological conditions, among other factors. Not only is the weather responsible for producing sufficient precipitation in the form of snow, it also influences the stability of the snowcover. Though mountain weather is very complex, a little basic knowledge and experience will help you to assess the avalanche danger level by observing a number of indicators. Changing weather conditions leave clues on the snowpack that may be read and interpreted by an alert freeskier. This allows you to judge whether the avalanche bulletin is applicable to the particular area where you are riding.

Rain, snow, wind, temperature and solar radiation are elements of weather that determine the avalanche danger level, together with terrain features and the human factor.

New Snow and Avalanche Hazard

> **Basic rule: New snow increases avalanche danger.**

Any change in the avalanche hazard depends on the type of new snow, temperature, wind speed and snow on the ground. The decisive factor is the intensity of snowfall — that is, the amount of snow in relation to time.

The basic rule is, **The faster snow is deposited, the higher the hazard**. A certain amount of new snow makes freeriding a very high-risk pleasure. When the **critical amount of new snow** (Munter Method) is reached, the avalanche hazard is **Considerable** (Level 3) or higher. Exercise extreme caution when new snow levels reach or exceed the critical amount.

Under **favorable conditions**, the danger level may not change or may increase slightly as new snow starts to accumulate.

Favorable conditions are:

> Low wind, or little wind loading
> Rain turning to snow
> Temperatures around freezing, particularly when snowfall starts
> Highly frequented slopes (riding and skiing stabilizes the snowpack.)

However, even in these favorable conditions, the avalanche danger level will increase significantly when the amount of new snow exceeds 12 to 25 inches (30–60 cm).

Unfavorable conditions include:

> High winds
> Temperatures below 13 degrees Fahrenheit (-8 degrees Celsius)
> New snow falling on surface hoar, crust, ice or very old snow
> Rarely frequented slopes in the backcountry

When new snow falls in unfavorable conditions, the critical amount of new snow may be reached with as little as 4–8 inches (10–20 cm) of snow, and in some conditions even less snow is necessary.

In a neutral situation, when favorable as well as unfavorable conditions are present, danger is to be expected whenever new snow accumulations reach eight to 12 inches (20–30 cm).

A higher avalanche danger level will prevail for the next several days, until the snow has sufficiently settled. Always be aware of an increased avalanche danger level when there is new snow.

Heavy snowfalls favor fast settling, as the weight of the snow soon consolidates the snowpack. In the short term, however, heavy snowfalls will increase the avalanche danger level drastically. High amounts of new snow are initially dangerous but soon form deep and stable snowcovers.

>> **The first beautiful day after an extended period of storms is particularly dangerous. Exercise extreme caution, be aware of all danger indicators and play safe in doubtful situations, even if that means avoiding a very tempting ride.**

🕿 Andi Schwarz

△ Turkey

⚐ Holger Feist,
   René Margreiter

Wind and Avalanche Hazard

Snow is the building block of the avalanche, but wind is the architect. Wind creates slabs and sets traps for unwary freeskiers. Wind loading occurs when snow is removed from windward slopes (areas facing the wind) and deposited on leeward slopes. During snowfall, the wind transports the snow and generally deposits it in places where the wind force is less strong. Therefore particularly large amounts of dangerous windblown snow can usually be found on the lee side of ridges, mountains and other terrain obstacles. Wind often blows at high speed in the mountains, so it is not surprising that wind may transport large amounts of snow. The higher the wind speed, the more snow is removed and deposited in areas of wind deceleration.

During snowfall the amount of windblown snow depends on the power of the wind: Moderate wind (15 mph/24 km/h) is a wind that you can feel, a wind that would fully move a handkerchief. Moderate wind creates wind-loaded areas with twice the depth of the new snowfall. Strong wind (30 mph/48 km/h) creates a "singing" noise in the trees, cables and wires and is painful on uncovered skin surfaces. Strong wind creates wind-loaded areas with triple the depth of the new fallen snow. Stormy wind (45 mph/72 km/h) is violent and makes a good deal of noise. It breaks tree branches and often creates plumes of snow coming off peaks and ridges. Stormy wind means heavy wind loading on all aspects of the mountain.

Wind loading increases dramatically with rising wind speed, but only to a point. When winds become too strong (faster than 50 miles per hour), the snow tends to remain suspended in the air and it sublimates away or is deposited farther downslope.

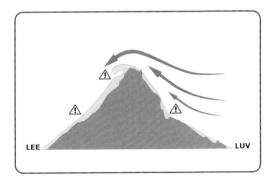

LEE   LUV

On windward slopes, the snowpack is usually more shallow than on the sheltered lee side, where deep layers of windblown snow (slabs) are deposited. But wind loading also occurs on windward slopes, particularly below steep sections and in gullies and depressions. The flatter the windward side, the more snow is transported to the lee side. The steeper the windward slope, the greater the accumulation of dangerous wind-loaded snow will be on the windward side.

Wind loading means avalanche hazard!

Prevailing winds are high-level winds blowing across mountain ranges. At ground level, wind direction is modified by terrain features and must be determined by observing clues on the snow surface.

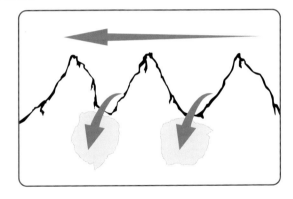

Wind transforms snow and creates cohesive slabs. In large parts of the United States and Canada (and also in Europe), prevailing winds blow from a westerly direction (west, northwest or southwest). Therefore wind loading is most common on east-facing slopes. Some areas may have more than one prevailing wind direction. Additionally, local winds that are mainly responsible for wind deposition depend on terrain features and several other factors and may blow from entirely different directions than prevailing winds. This means that even if snowfall is brought by westerly winds, there is no guarantee that wind loading will be limited to east-facing slopes.

Heavy snowfall combined with wind leads to dangerous wind loading on all slopes.

Luckily the snow surface provides a number of clues that help determine wind direction on a particular slope.

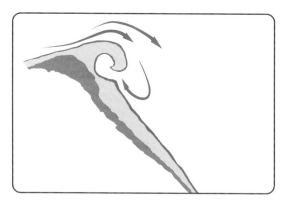

Large amounts of windblown snow have increased this slope's angle. Toward the bottom, the snowpack has become more shallow and therefore less stable. Beware of remote triggering! The cornice may break off if additional stresses are applied.

Cornices overhang dangerous lee slopes. The cornice always points into the direction where snow was deposited by the wind. Below the cornice is an extremely dangerous snow pillow that consists of a large amount of wind blown snow in the steepest section of the slope.

The shallow snowpack on the bottom of the slope is under compression stresses caused by the large masses of snow in higher sections. Remote triggering may occur in these weak areas at the bottom, leaving very slim chances for escape.

Even though cornices may sometimes appear very solid, they are a sign of imminent danger!

Wind ripples and dunes on the snow surface are indicators of wind transport. Strong winds can deposit large amounts of snow. Ripples can reach a depth of up to one yard (one meter). The illustration below shows a cross section of these ripples with the wind blowing at a right angle. Wind ripples and dunes run perpendicular to the direction of the wind.

Wind transforms snow and creates cohesive slabs that may be prone to release. Wind ripples and dunes are a warning sign for avalanche hazard.

Wind ripples and dunes run perpendicular to the direction of the wind; the steep side of the dune is on its lee side. Dunes mean wind loading and an accumulation of windblown snow: Danger!

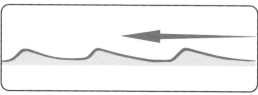

Wind deposition created the large unstable slab that preceded this avalanche. Wind loading occurred from bottom left to top right.
☞Swiss Federal Institute for Snow and Avalanche Research, FISAR

Sastrugi are the result of wind etching or **erosion** of the snow surface. Unlike ripples, the steep faces of sastrugi are on the windward side — they face the wind. They are often very hard and rather unpleasant to ride on. If you see sastrugi, ask yourself where all the windblown snow has been deposited.

Strong wind has etched sastrugi into the snowcover. The hardest layers resisted the wind. The steep faces of sastrugi always point in the direction of the wind.

Sastrugi on a wind-exposed ridge.

☞Richard Walch △ Arlberg, Austria

Blow holes often form around rocks or other terrain features. They are caused by the scouring action of eddies that remove snow around these obstacles.

Drift tails are long, narrow tail-shaped mounds of snow deposited by wind on the lee side of obstacles. Drift tails are a sure indication of wind direction.

Windblown ridges and slope sections exposed to strong winds are often bare, even in midwinter. Wind blows across them at accelerated speeds, picks up snow on the windward side and deposits it in gullies, small bowls and other depressions. Don't be misguided and think that the snowpack is generally shallow and that the avalanche hazard is therefore low. Under these conditions, **channels** and **gullies** can be extremely dangerous. They are filled with very unstable windblown snow ready to release as slab avalanches. Wind-loaded gullies are particularly dangerous, because even relatively small amounts of snow can bury a skier many feet (several meters) deep. In steep gullies, even minor loose-snow avalanches, or sluffs, can be extremely nasty, sweeping a rider downhill. If there is an avalanche in a gully, you have little chance of getting out.

The **Chinook**, and its European equivalent, the **Foehn**, are both warm dry winds blowing on the lee side of mountain ranges. They can reach high speeds and cause significant wind loading. They also have a great influence on local weather. A Chinook or Foehn not only warms the air as it passes down a mountain range but also pushes back the cold arctic air, thus causing a substantial rise in temperature. This effect may increase the avalanche hazard and makes snow melt away at a fast rate, hence the Native American name **snow eater**.

   These strong winds lead to rapid loading of leeward slopes. While a Chinook or Foehn usually blows in a certain direction, all variations are possible (due to terrain deviations), and the situation must be individually assessed in order to identify dangerous wind slabs.

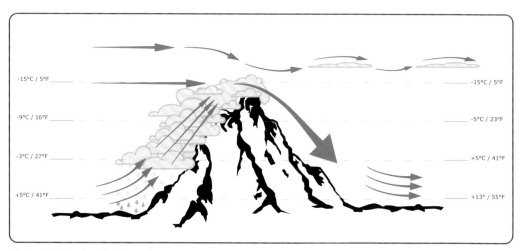

Foehn / Chinook – the Snow Eater.
A (relatively) warm and strong wind. A Foehn is caused when a storm (low pressure area) leads to cloud buildup at the windward side of a mountain range resulting in strong precipitation. Moist air is lifted, loses its moisture and cools down (approx. 0.5°C/100m). The loss of precipitation dries the air and as it descends on the lee side it is warmed by compression (approx. 1°C/100m). This often results in warm and windy conditions and thawing of the snowpack on the lee side of the mountain range. Foehn winds can be caused by any mountain range regardless of geographic location. In some areas of North America these warm winds are called a Chinook.

The Foehn in Austria's Arlberg region.
Blue sky with only a few lenticular clouds
indicates strong winds aloft. The Foehn (here a
strong southerly wind) often deposits large
amounts of snow, particularly in leeward slopes.

⌾Richard Walch △ Arlberg, Austria

Wind-packed windward slope. The wind has set
a series of traps in this slope. Note signs of wind
influence on the snow surface. The almost bare
ridge tops indicate even worse wind loading on
the lee side.

⌾Thorsten Indra △ New Mexico

Snow plumes visible on ridge tops in clear weather indicate strong winds at higher
altitude. Don't confuse snow plumes with clouds! Remember that very strong winds may
cause large plumes of blowing snow, but that moderate to strong winds cause the most
wind loading and slab formation. Just like the Foehn or Chinook, these gales that create
snow plumes can be very strong and deposit large amounts of snow on leeward slopes.

A storm in clear weather conditions.
Plumes of snow streaming off the ridge
tops indicate high winds and intense
snow transport. Even without new snow
falling, large amounts of windblown
snow create dangerous slabs.

⌾Bernhard Spöttel △ Kamtchatka, Russia

Solar Radiation and Temperature. Solar radiation and temperature are closely connected, so it's no surprise that they both influence avalanche hazard. As mentioned before, the amount of solar radiation a slope receives depends on its orientation and angle relative to the low winter sun. Even in midwinter, with air temperatures below zero, you may be basking on a sunny slope that receives particularly strong radiation because the slope directly faces the low winter sun. Settlement and metamorphosis strongly depend on temperature. Therefore, south-facing slopes stabilize faster through rounding and melt-freeze metamorphosis than less sunny aspects (northwest-, north-, northeast- or east-facing slopes).

The amount of heat energy a slope receives depends on the angle of solar radiation relative to the slope. Slopes inclined toward the sun receive the most heat. On level ground, heat's intensity is reduced due to the radiation's low angle and distribution over a larger area. Steep north-facing slopes are not exposed to any solar radiation in midwinter.

Shady slopes typically have a large temperature gradient between the relatively warm ground surface (around the freezing point) and the cold snow surface (many degrees below freezing), which favors the formation of faceted snow and depth hoar and causes dangerous instability.

North-facing slopes may produce thick layers of surface hoar in midwinter. Since these slopes do not receive any solar radiation during that period, these layers remain intact and become extremely dangerous gliding surfaces if covered by subsequent snowfall. In high alpine areas, the wind will often destroy those fragile crystals, while they may persist and become buried in sheltered areas such as forest glades. Steep shady slopes facing northwest, north, northeast or east are the most dangerous areas for freeriding and freeskiing. Don't be lured into a trap by the perfect powder you may find in these slopes.

Latitude, Solar Radiation and Avalanche Hazard

If we observe the sun's course across the sky, we notice that during winter it moves lower above the southern horizon (assuming you are somewhere in the Northern Hemisphere). On December 21, the sun reaches its lowest point. After that date, the hours of daylight increase as the sun rises higher above the horizon. On June 21, the longest day, it reaches its highest position and then apparently begins to sink again.

In lower latitudes (in the United States except Alaska, in southern Canada and in the European Alps), the sun is higher in the sky than it is in higher latitudes farther north of the equator.

North of 55 degrees, there is little daylight in midwinter. In late winter the sun reappears, daylight returns and the intensity of solar radiation increases. By late spring, daylight lasts a lot longer at higher latitudes and the snowpack receives more radiation than it does farther south.

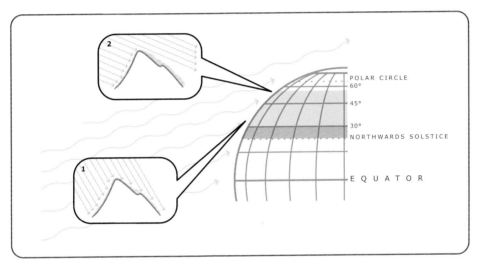

POLAR CIRCLE
60°

45°

30°
NORTHWARDS SOLSTICE

E Q U A T O R

Latitude, Solar Radiation and the Snowpack.
As we move north from the equator, the angle of incoming solar radiation becomes increasingly flatter and intensifies the effects of a slope's orientation.
1. In lower latitudes, solar energy is distributed fairly evenly over all slope aspects due to the high angle at which the sun's rays hit the surface.
2. In the north, solar radiation arrives at a lower angle, which reduces the overall amount of energy. Nevertheless, sunny slopes receive a lot of thermal energy. North-facing slopes are not exposed to any direct solar radiation in winter.

Climate, Snowpack and Avalanche Hazard

The avalanche danger level is subject to geographic location, time and weather parameters. The general climate of a region plays a major role in snowpack stability and its general characteristics. According to prevailing climatic conditions, we can roughly distinguish the following snowpack types:

> Cool Humid Climate — Maritime Snowpack (influenced by oceans)

Areas that receive high amounts of precipitation at relatively mild winter temperatures are usually characterized by deep and stable snowpacks. Snow depths are commonly around a minimum of 100 inches (three meters) and more. Such conditions can be found in coastal mountain ranges. Precipitation here is frequent and significant, as moist air from the ocean cools as it passes over the mountains and is forced to loose a lot of its moisture. Rain is also common, and wet-snow avalanches occur throughout the winter.

The snowpack on coastal mountains tends to be deep and rather homogenous and stable. Avalanches generally release naturally during storms or immediately after storms (direct-action avalanches). Danger is usually not persistent over extended periods of time after storms, since the usually moist and heavy snow bonds well with old snow at mild temperatures. Weak layers often occur in new snow caused by temperature changes during a storm. Also, weak layers tend to occur on top of ice crusts caused by rain or sun. In favorable conditions, it is possible to ride or ski even very steep slopes that are not rideable on the less stable, shallow continental snowpacks. Nevertheless, the basic rule — the more new snow, the higher the avalanche hazard — also applies in the maritime areas, especially when the new snow falls on a slick, icy crust.

>>>Warning! Even in areas with deep and stable snowpacks, there may be hidden avalanche dangers. Faceted snow may form in the early season when the snowpack is shallow and temperatures cold. Likewise surface hoar will form during dry periods.

Maritime snowpacks can be found in the Cascade Mountains (Oregon and Washington) and in the Coast Ranges of Alaska and British Columbia.

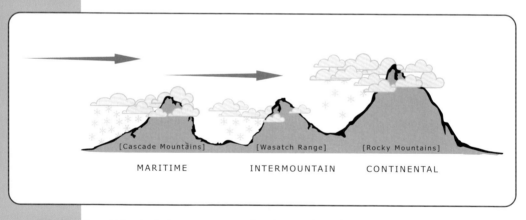

[Cascade Mountains]   [Wasatch Range]   [Rocky Mountains]

MARITIME   INTERMOUNTAIN   CONTINENTAL

A storm (e.g., the cold front of a low pressure area) on its way from the Pacific Ocean to the Rocky Mountains. The first and heaviest snowfalls occur in the Cascade Mountains. Mountain ranges further to the east still receive considerable (though already lower) amounts of precipitation. By the time the clouds reach the Rocky Mountains they have lost most of their humidity. The amount of (usually very dry) snow is relatively low.

Rough classification of North American snow climates:
1. **Coastal areas** with generally deep snowpacks (maritime climate).
2. **Intermountain areas** are neither continental nor maritime climates. Depending on the area, these climates may either be predominantly maritime (deep snowpacks) or continental (shallow snowpacks) or something in between.
3. **Continental Areas** – dry and cold climate with often shallow and unstable snow-packs.

Warning: These snowpack-zones frequently shift and represent local irregularities.

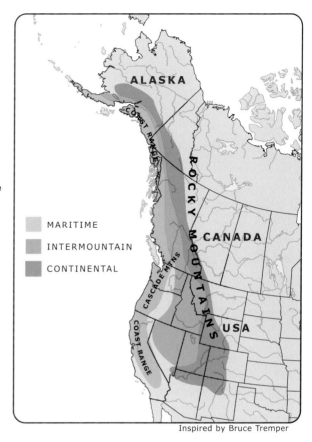

MARITIME

INTERMOUNTAIN

CONTINENTAL

Inspired by Bruce Tremper

> Cold Dry Climate — Continental Snowpack (far from the influence of oceans)

Far from the oceans is the continental zone, where the snowpack is thinner than that of wet maritime areas. This shallow snowpack, generally less than 70 inches (two meters), is often dangerous!

Continental climates are characterized by cold, sunny and, unfortunately, rather dry weather. By the time a storm reaches a continental mountain range, it has already lost most of its moisture to other mountain ranges along the way. Snow is therefore usually dry and light. With a bit of luck, freeriders can find some of that legendary perfect powder.

>> **Warning!** Prolonged periods of low temperatures (0 to -20 degrees Fahrenheit, or -18 to -30 degrees Celsius) and a shallow snowpack is a dangerous combination that should ring the alarm bells in every skier's head. The shallow snowpack is often like a house of cards; it rests on a weak base of faceted snow and may possess a multitude of other hidden weak layers.

Depth hoar is extremely common here. Surface hoar is common, especially at middle elevations. At high elevations, strong winds inhibit its formation. Massive powder dumps and rain are rare. The unstable snowpack is particularly dangerous for boarders and skiers who succumb to the irresistible temptation of "champagne" powder. Continental areas such as the Colorado Rockies and the Central European Alps lead the statistics of avalanche deaths. Unstable foundations of faceted snow are almost the rule in these areas. Early and mid winter are the most dangerous seasons. In late winter, milder temperatures and higher snow levels put an end to the formation of depth hoar. If the snowpack is reasonably deep and well settled, it may provide acceptable conditions for freeriding even with a foundation of faceted snow. However, when the snowpack thaws for the first time in spring and becomes water saturated all the way down to the faceted layers, the underlying base becomes even more precarious and large slab avalanches are to be expected.

Compared with areas with heavy snowfalls, avalanches in continental climates may occur many days after the last storm. Weak layers are long lasting. (Avalanches in March may occur on weak layers that formed in November.) Also, because of the depth hoar and surface hoar, avalanches can be triggered in flat areas at the bottom of steep slopes, just like pulling a log out from the bottom of a woodpile. In addition to Colorado and Central Europe, examples of continental climates include parts of the Canadian Rockies.

> Mixed Climate — Intermountain Snowpack (intermediate influence of oceans)

Mixed climates combine the characteristic elements of both continental and maritime areas. Precipitation and snowpack levels are subject to local variations. Storms tend to be more frequent and with more snow than those affecting the continental zones, so snowpack depths range from 50 to 100 inches (1.5–3 meters). Also, temperatures in the mixed climate are warmer than those in continental areas but colder than those in maritime climates. Depth and stability of the snowpack depend on temperature and precipitation patterns through the winter, and snowpacks may either be deep and stable, shallow and weak, or anything in between the two extremes.

⊕ Richard Walch

△ Red Mountain, Canada

⌾ Billy Summers

Instability often results from weak layers that form in shallow snowpacks during the early season and during periods of dry and mild weather, which usually bring surface hoar. Faceted snow can also form near the surface, only to be buried later by future storms. Examples of intermountain zones are the Wasatch Range in Utah and parts of the Selkirk Range in British Columbia.

> The Snowpack in High Northern Latitudes

Jeff Curtes △ Valdez, Alaska

In the far north and Arctic regions, the snowpack tends to be less stable than that of more southern latitudes. However, it is again important to consider whether a maritime (cool and humid) or a continental (cold and dry) influence prevails. Likewise the snowpack on a big mountain will vary with elevation. The snowpack of the Alaska Range, for instance, may be deep and quite stable where it is exposed to the influence of the ocean, while it may be relatively shallow and subject to strong faceting in the more continental areas farther inland.

The climate becomes more severe north of the Arctic Circle (latitudes greater than 66 degrees). Solar radiation is extremely low in these areas in the winter, and north of the

Arctic Circle, the sun is totally invisible over an extended period of time. In many areas the ground remains frozen year-round (permafrost), and temperatures remain extremely low for the largest part of winter.

Spring is a short period that comes late in the year, but it is characterized by intense warming that causes rapid thawing of the snowpack. Avalanche activity increases quickly as water-saturated snow begins to slide on the impermeable permafrost ground and flows down to the valleys. Called slush flows, these avalanches occur on relatively flat terrain (5 degrees to 25 degrees). This type of avalanche occurs only in the sparsely populated far north and rarely claims lives.

>> **Warning!** This is only a general division of climatic types that should not be overrated. Mixed forms of climatic conditions and snowpack characteristics occur as a rule. In dry winters, a usually deep and stable maritime snowpack, for instance, may exhibit characteristics similar to those of a continental snowpack.

In early winter most areas tend to have shallow and unstable snowpacks (continental features) no matter how close or far from the ocean they may be.

It is easy to keep track of weather patterns in your local ski or freeride area by accessing information on the Internet. This is a fast and easy way to find out whether to expect a shallow and unstable or deep and stable snowpack. Of course, you always have to determine whether the information is correct — no secondhand information is as good as firsthand information. **Know your snow!**

Remember the following rules of thumb:

> **Consistently low temperatures keep the hazard high** over extended periods of time!
  Low temperatures slow down rounding and, therefore, the settling of the snowpack.
  When the snow is shallow, faceting may occur and further contribute to instability.
> **A slow and moderate rise in temperature** together with dry snow conditions reduces
  the avalanche hazard as it **favors settling and reduces stresses** in the snowpack.
> **A rapid and substantial rise** in temperature due to warm weather, warm winds (foehn,
  Chinook) and rain **raises the hazard** in the short term.
> **Rising temperature after** snowfall at **low temperatures** raises the **hazard**.
> **Melt-freeze cycles** stabilize a snowpack. Melt-freeze cycles, typical of spring weather,
  provide safe conditions in the morning, when the snowpack is still frozen.
  For good skiing conditions, temperatures must drop sufficiently during the night to
  create a **solid crust** that supports a rider's weight. Avalanche hazard rises during
  daytime as the snowpack begins to thaw in the sun.

>> Chapter 3 : Danger Evaluation

"No risk, no fun. But without boundaries you're dead."

Werner Munter, avalanche expert

Richard Walch △ Arlberg, Austria Martin Rutz

: Fun Without Risk: Is It Possible?

Freeriding is an inherently dangerous sport. Every rider consciously or unconsciously accepts the risk of being caught in an avalanche, falling off a cliff or being injured in other ways. Until the mid '90s, there was no suitable method for quickly evaluating a slope's avalanche danger. Snow pits and stability tests proved unsuitable for quickly assessing local danger. One example is the glide block test, or *rutschblock*, which involves adding weight (of people) onto a section (block) of the slope until a shear fracture happens and the section starts to slide. (See Glossary in Chapter 9.) The results of these tests could simply not be applied to other sections of the same slope, much less other slopes. Terrible avalanche accidents were the consequence. The practical application of avalanche knowledge had run into a dead end. The weak spot of all these methods was that the results gave information only about the examined site and said little about a slope's overall stability.

In search of something that was quick and easy to learn, **Werner Munter** developed the **3x3 Filter** and **Reduction methods**. This new approach allows individual risk management, letting each rider or skier decide how much risk he or she wants to take without requiring an expert's knowledge of snow metamorphosis or snow pits.

The main elements of this modern approach are the current **avalanche bulletin**, and **assessments** of the **snow surface**, the **terrain** and the **human factors**. These elements are used to determine whether or not avalanche risk in a given situation is acceptable.

However, there is always risk. No method can ever be 100 percent safe, especially in high snow-covered mountains.

This chapter forms the backbone of this book, because these methods can bring you **safely** through the winter. This is **avalanche knowledge** that **works** in the field. Take your time to learn the methods presented in this chapter and participate in a practical avalanche course or freeride camp. You will see that maximum safety and great fun are compatible. As you develop these important skills, you'll see that you can enjoy freeriding even more!

>> Note that the 3x3 Filter and Reduction methods presented in this book are the cutting edge of European avalanche safety and are currently (2003) not taught in most North American avalanche schools. However, we are sure that you will find any good avalanche course rewarding and beneficial, as it provides you with the necessary skill base for applying the 3x3 Filter Method and the Reduction Method.

: Instability Clues

The most reliable means for avoiding avalanche accidents is recognizing and correctly interpreting clues provided by the snow surface. Even though slab avalanches are extremely treacherous, there are often clear and unmistakable warning signs. All you need to do is learn how to recognize them.

Cracks in the snowpack are signs of imminent danger.

⊕ Stefan Schütz   △ Arlberg, Austria   🏂 Thomas Wyden

Remember the following warning signs:

> Natural release of snow slabs (not caused by skiers and snowboarders or by explosives)

> Remote release of snow slabs

> Hollow whumpfing noises, which are often the last warning

(These sounds are created when air escapes from a collapsing snowpack. If the fracture is limited to a thin surface layer, you may hear a clear hissing noise.)

> Cracks appearing on the snow surface

> Large amounts of recently deposited windblown snow

> Ripples and dunes on the snow surface

> Water-saturated snowpack

> Avalanche-control measures (explosives) and closed-down ski trails

People: Avalanche triggers

Almost all fatal avalanches are triggered by the victims themselves. Avalanche accidents and people who trigger their own avalanches are inseparable phenomena. When we are out riding, we tend to ignore danger and share the common belief that it is always someone else who gets caught in a slide. This **"it'll-be-all-right"** attitude is pure nonsense and dangerous negligence. Anybody who ignores obvious hazards takes a stupid risk.

This rider triggered an avalanche. He reacted quickly, and with a lot of luck he was able to hold onto a rock.

⊙Richard Walch △ Arlberg, Austria ⚲Tommy Brunner

Not every rider triggers a slide on a dangerous slope. There is a big difference between an experienced rider who carefully picks a sensible line and a group of careless beginners who bomb a slope. But you have the opportunity to reduce your risk by observing the following principles:

> Hiking puts stresses of two to three times the weight of your body on the snowpack.
> Riding doubles the stresses of hiking. Turns result in particularly high stresses.
> Snowboarders apply lower additional loads on the snowpack than skiers do.
> A fall increases stresses by a factor of seven. That means around half a ton of additional load!
> Jumps over cliffs or cornices increase stresses by a factor of 10!
> Snowmobiles always put extremely high stresses (far more than 850 pounds per square yard) on the snowpack. (It is not possible to lessen the stress induced by a snowmobile by riding it carefully.)

Unless conditions are very stable (which is rarely the case), you should always ease the stress when hiking by maintaining a safe distance between individual skiers and riders in your group. On steep sections, the minimum safe distance is 45 to 60 feet (15 to 20 meters); on particularly dangerous sections, you should go one at a time.

On steep slopes, always ride one at a time; it is more enjoyable and much safer.

For out-of-bounds, the basic rule is:

"The snowpack is a fragile structure; handle it with great care." —Werner Munter

: Peer Pressure

Group dynamics and peer pressure can often be deadly. People who take risks often receive more respect in a group. We usually assume that other people know what they are doing, and we hesitate to come forward with doubts because we don't want to be a sissy. ("It must be safe, because if it weren't safe, somebody would surely say something.") This attitude is extremely dangerous, but we all have it. All group members must be involved in decision making, because groups possess more knowledge and resources than does any single individual. On the other hand, groups always take higher risks than individuals. Within a group we tend to feel safe and underestimate risks. Therefore you should not blindly trust the top dog, even if he or she is your best friend. If you feel uncomfortable, your intuition is trying to warn you. Don't ignore that feeling! This rule is particularly true — and difficult to enforce — if the de facto leader makes important route decisions by just being out front.

"In life-threatening situations, your belly is often more reliable than your head. When you've got that bad feeling in your gut, you know that this is not your day. Go with your gut, even if your head is trying to tell you something else and your buddies are laughing at you. It's better to be chicken and survive than to be a hero and die!" (Werner Munter)

> It isn't the strong but the weak who ride every slope, even if those slopes are obviously dangerous. It takes real strength to avoid a promising ride.

: Particularly Dangerous Aspects —
Northwest, North, Northeast and East

> **East-facing slopes: Northeast, East, Southeast**
> East-facing slopes are often sheltered from the wind and subject to wind loading. Large amounts of windblown snow on east-facing slopes are responsible for a high number of fatal accidents.

> **North-facing slopes: Northwest, North, Northeast**
> North-facing slopes are in the shade most of the time. Low temperatures together with scarce solar radiation preserve dangerous conditions over extended periods of time. Layers of surface hoar may form in these areas and later be buried under subsequent snowfalls. Formation of depth hoar frequently causes further instability. Around 60 percent of fatal accidents occur in north-facing slopes.

> **Shaded forest glades**
> While surface hoar often gets destroyed by wind in the alpine zone before it can be buried by snowfalls, it often persists in steep forest glades, where the powder stays light for a long time. If you think there could be buried surface hoar, avoid the glades. Getting caught in an avalanche is particularly dangerous in the trees!

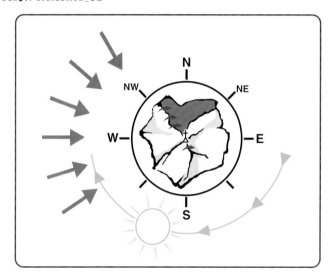

Shady slopes (those facing northwest, north or northeast) can be extremely dangerous. The snowpack there is often very unstable because of sugar snow, buried surface hoar and scarce solar radiation. Lee slopes (those facing northeast, east or southeast) are often filled with dangerous windblown snow, particularly after a snowfall and/or high winds.

On south-facing slopes, high solar radiation, sintering and/or compaction result in a more stable snowpack. After a big snowfall, natural avalanches can release on any slope, regardless of its aspect. Also, beware of wet-snow avalanches on a slope exposed to strong solar radiation and warm temperatures. Windward slopes (those facing west and west-northwest) may also contain wind slabs, therefore check each individual slope.

Around 75 percent of fatal avalanche accidents occur on slopes facing northwest, north or east.

Distribution of fatal accidents according to slope aspect.

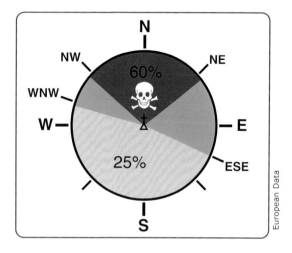

European Data

The north sector (northwest to northeast) is the deadly zone, with 60 percent of all fatalities. The northern half (west-northwest to east-southeast) claims three quarters of all victims. Avoiding these aspects in unstable conditions can save your life. The sunny side (southeast to southwest) is statistically much safer, but always check the risk! (Don't become one of the few avalanche victims in these aspects!)

Typical Avalanche Terrain

Typical avalanche terrain is a very steep lee slope after recent snowfall. Slab avalanches release especially often on steep, rocky slopes (those steeper than 39 degrees) in sections around the rocks.

A suspected avalanche-prone slope with large amounts of windblown snow.

Reiner Pickl △ Arlberg, Austria

The Avalanche Bulletin

The avalanche bulletin (we will use the abbreviation AB in this chapter) provides information on the current avalanche danger level and expected conditions for safety personnel, freeriders, freeskiers and other individuals who travel in the backcountry — in short, for all those who are exposed to avalanche hazard in their work or in leisure activities. Together with longboard or powder skis, the AB is a freerider's most important basic tool.

The AB is often posted in ski area lodges, huts, some hotels and police stations. It is also available by fax and telephone and on the Internet. For useful addresses and phone numbers in the United States and Canada, see Chapter 9 and www. POWDERGUIDE .com.

The current avalanche danger level for a given area is based on information collected by experts at various locations. These experts record data such as the amount of new snow, depth of the snowpack, temperature and wind speed, and they regularly dig snow pits and perform rutschblock tests to gather information on the composition of the snowpack and its stability. Based on this data, the avalanche information centers publish their avalanche bulletins. The United States, Canada and Europe all use a danger rating system that distinguishes five levels of avalanche danger based on the stability of the snowpack and probability of triggering a slide.

Apart from the current danger level, the AB usually contains the following information:

> An overview of the weather (new snow, wind, temperature, solar radiation) and its effects on the snowpack
> Composition of the snowpack, particularly weak layers, stability and settlement
> Particularly dangerous areas and aspects; sometimes additional information on the probability of triggering a slide on critical slopes
> Outlook on the expected development of the avalanche danger level
> Tips for backcountry travelers — what slopes to avoid

How to Use the Avalanche Bulletin

The AB roughly distinguishes between areas of favorable and unfavorable conditions. Just like the weather report, it is a **prognosis** of expected conditions. There is always a chance that this prognosis may be wrong. The accuracy and quality of the avalanche bulletin de-pends on the number of field observers and weather stations and other resources avail-able to forecasters. The AB might not tell you which slopes are dangerous, only that there may be dangerous slopes in areas of unfavorable conditions. Keep in mind, how-ever, that the number of actually dangerous slopes rises with the danger level. Therefore, the higher the danger level, the greater your chance of hitting a weak spot on a danger-ous slope.

The AB is a valuable source of information for freeriders, but it provides only a general guideline, because it assesses avalanche danger for a wide area. The actual danger may change within a few yards (meters), therefore the AB can **never** tell you that a **particular slope** is stable. The AB may be wrong, and since it is a forecast, it can never be as accurate (or as up-to-date) as your own observations. Therefore, always **keep your eyes open!**

 It is always up to you to decide whether or not to ride a slope. It's your own life that is at stake!

U.S. Avalanche Danger Rating

Each AB is organized into the following sections:

> **Avalanche Probability and Avalanche Trigger**
> **Degree and Distribution of Avalanche Danger**
> **Recommended Action in the Backcountry**

Or:

> **WHAT ... is happening in the snow?**
> **WHY ... is this happening?**
> **WHERE ... are the most dangerous slopes and areas?**
> **WHAT TO DO ... to have fun and avoid an avalanche.**

▪ LOW

Natural avalanches very unlikely. Human-triggered avalanches unlikely. Generally stable snow. Isolated areas of instability. Travel is generally safe. Normal caution is advised.

▪ MODERATE

Natural avalanches unlikely. Human-triggered avalanches possible. Unstable slabs possible on steep terrain. Use caution on steeper terrain with certain aspects (defined in the accompanying statement).

▪ CONSIDERABLE

Natural avalanches possible. Human-triggered avalanches probable. Unstable slabs probable on steep terrain. Be increasingly cautious on steeper terrain.

▪ HIGH

Natural and human-triggered avalanches likely. Unstable slabs likely for a variety of aspects and slope angles. Travel in avalanche terrain is not recommended. Safest travel on windward ridges of lower-angle slopes without steeper terrain above.

▪ EXTREME

Widespread natural or human-triggered avalanches certain. Extremely unstable slabs certain for most aspects and slope angles. Large, destructive avalanches possible. Travel in avalanche terrain should be avoided and travel confined to low-angle terrain well away from avalanche-path runouts.

The avalanche bulletin usually contains a more detailed description of dangerous areas (e.g., elevation, aspect and terrain). Below is a definition of terms frequently used in the AB:

Additional loads:

> high   (e.g., a group of skiers not keeping a safety distance; snow cats)
> low   (e.g., an individual skier or hiker)

Terrain:

> Moderately steep terrain   slopes with an inclination of less than 30 degrees
> Steep slopes   steeper than approximately 30 degrees
> Extremely steep slopes   particularly dangerous areas with regard to inclination and terrain features
> Aspect   slope orientation looking down the fall line
> Exposed   particularly exposed to danger
> Natural release   without human involvement

> This danger rating corresponds to systems in place all over Europe, the United States and Canada.

For more on the Canadian and the more detailed European danger rating systems, see Chapter 9.

: Interpretation of the Avalanche Bulletin

>> The only safe place is at home...

> > **Low Danger** means generally stable conditions. High additional loads (e.g., a group of freeriders or skiers) may still trigger avalanches on extremely steep terrain.

>> Fairly favorable...

> > **Moderate Danger** means predominantly good conditions. Caution is required in areas of increased danger as defined in the AB. High additional loads (e.g., a group of freeriders or skiers or a single snowmobile) may trigger avalanches. A single rider may trigger a slide on steep slopes with a very unstable snowpack.

>> Often good powder but risky...

> > **Considerable Danger** (critical situation) means that the avalanche danger level is twice as high as in Moderate Danger. Because of partially unfavorable conditions and often hidden dangers, the situation is critical. The snowpack is unstable on many steep slopes. Highly dangerous areas are indicated in the AB. Human release by individual skiers is probable; natural release (without additional loads) is possible. Large avalanches may release and advance onto flat terrain. Remote release is possible from the bottom of a slope. Since remote release is possible, approach the steepest slope sections with caution. Whumpfing sounds are frequent and indicate danger. Take full advantage of good route finding and islands of safety for ascent and descent. **Avoid steep rocky slopes. Reduce stresses to a minimum by avoiding jumps over cliffs and cornices. Snowmobile use in these conditions is playing avalanche roulette.**

>> A good day to die in an avalanche...

> > **High Danger** means very unstable conditions and imminent avalanche danger. The danger level is twice as high again as that of Considerable. The snowpack is unstable, and steep slopes are dangerous in all aspects. Natural avalanches can be large and are likely to move onto flat terrain and overcome obstacles, such as mounds and walls. Remote releases from faraway points are likely. Stay in flat terrain (an inclination of less than 30 degrees) or on patrolled trails (within the avalanche-controlled boundaries of ski areas). Backcountry touring is only possible in hilly terrain (less than 30 degrees). Stay clear of avalanche runout zones.

>> Freeriding? Forget it!

> > **Extreme Danger** means emergency alert. Exposed villages and roads are in danger. Don't even think about riding or skiing. Wait for the situation to return to normal.

Around 30 percent of all fatal accidents occur at Moderate Danger and 60 percent at Considerable Danger. Only five percent of fatal accidents occur at Low Danger. High and Extreme Danger levels are responsible for around five percent of all fatalities. The reason for this is that the avalanche risk is very obvious on days of Extreme and High Danger. On the other hand, the risk is much more difficult to recognize at levels Moderate to Considerable. These two danger levels are very common on most winter days. The hazards are hidden and difficult to evaluate. In order to avoid traps, you must keep your eyes open and be able to avoid slopes that seem dangerous. If the avalanche bulletin seems inaccurate, act as if the danger rating is one level above the one indicated in the AB. Clear indicators of inaccurate ratings are:

> Changing weather (e.g., strong snowfall)
> You hear whumpfing sounds when the AB reports a Moderate Danger (the true danger level is probably Considerable)
> Remote triggering and natural avalanches, which mean that danger is at least Considerable if not High or Extreme

Average annual cumulative duration of the various danger levels (percentage of the entire winter). Note that there are only a few days of High and Extreme Danger

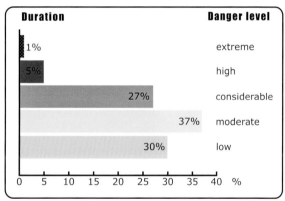

Swiss Federal Institute for Snow and Avalanche Research (FISAR) J. Schweizer and M. Lütsch, 2001.

The problem is that good snow conditions for freeriding often coincide with Considerable or High avalanche danger. Unfortunately there is no such thing as 15 inches (38 cm) of powder at Low Danger. This is why every freerider must make his or her own decision about whether the fun factors (powder and blue skies) acceptably outweigh the avalanche danger.

: Risk Management According to Werner Munter

⌨Richard Walch △ Aspen ⚲Oli Stolle

Smart freeriding and freeskiing for maximum safety — what you need and don't need:

> All you need is your own head — this is a "high brain, low tech" method
> You don't need any new equipment
> You don't need years of experience in mountain travel (what you do need is some
>   basic experience)
> You don't need to examine the snowpack, as the results are not applicable to other slopes

: The 3x3 Filter Method–
How to Assess Avalanche Danger

Swiss mountain guide, trainer and avalanche expert Werner Munter has developed a method that allows anyone going into the backcountry to drastically reduce the risk of triggering avalanches. The **3x3 Filter Method** aims to reduce existing risks to an acceptable minimum. This method is based on the principle that backcountry adventure can **never** be absolutely safe and that we are therefore forced to develop an awareness for potential danger.

In the backcountry, riders and skiers are exposed to avalanche danger that arises from the following three factors:

> Snow (snow and weather conditions)
> The mountain (terrain)
> Humans (anyone who wants to go up or down a slope)

If you overlook one of these factors, such as the possibility of triggering your own slide (the human factor), you are bound to make a terrible mistake with potentially deadly consequences!

It is completely irrelevant whether or not a slope is stable if no one is on that slope. What matters is whether that particular slope is stable enough for you to be on it. Therefore you must always consider the following three factors for the assessment of potential dangers in a given slope:

> 1. Snow and weather conditions
> 2. Terrain
> 3. Riders and skiers who want to be on that slope

If you only examine each slope for these factors, however, the remaining risk is still too high. If you don't want to play Russian roulette, you have to look at avalanche danger through a carefully focused **zoom lens**. This allows you to "filter out" 99 percent of the avalanche risk.

For that purpose we examine the three factors from three different perspectives:

> 1. Regional: Use weather reports and avalanche bulletins to gain information on conditions in the entire region and resulting dangers.
> 2. Local: Try to recognize possible dangers within your range of vision (consider using binoculars).
> 3. Zonal: Determine dangerous spots and potential risks on the slope and along the route you wish to take.

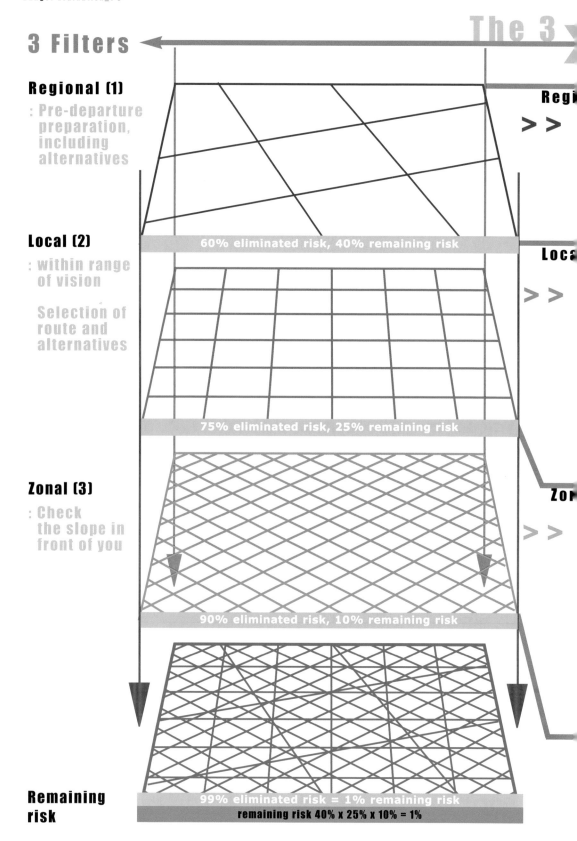

3 Filters

The 3

Regional (1)
: Pre-departure preparation, including alternatives

Regi

\>\>

Local (2)
: within range of vision

Selection of route and alternatives

60% eliminated risk, 40% remaining risk

Loca

\>\>

75% eliminated risk, 25% remaining risk

Zonal (3)
: Check the slope in front of you

Zo

\>\>

90% eliminated risk, 10% remaining risk

Remaining risk

99% eliminated risk = 1% remaining risk

remaining risk 40% x 25% x 10% = 1%

Method ➡ 3 Factors

1 Snow and Weather Conditions
- Avalanche bulletin
- Weather forecast
- Expert opinions and information

: assessment

2 Terrain
- A map with the largest scale available
- Guide-books, photos, air photos
- Personal knowledge of the terrain and area you will be traveling in

3 Human Factor
- Who is coming?
- Level of experience and skill
- Equipment
- Physical fitness, mental strength
- Is there a designated leader?

- External information • forecasts > • expectations

1 Snow and Weather Conditions
- Snow:
> Wind loading
> Signs of danger
> Critical amount of new snow
> Wind: ripples, dunes or sastrugi
> Is the AB correct? Make changes in case of doubt!
> Identify dangerous areas
- Weather:
> Visibility > Clouds > Wind speed
> Dangerous wind loading?
> Precipitation (amount of new snow)
> Temperature changes

2 Terrain
- Terrain features
> Slope angle
> Aspect(s)
- Are the tracks left by previous riders or skiers adapted to current terrain and current danger factors?

: evaluation

3 Human Factor
- Who are my companions?
- Check emergency equipment (transceivers, etc.)
- Are other groups traveling on the same route? (Discuss and coordinate plans with them, if helpful.)
- Time factor (remaining time): Are you on time? Or is it getting too late?

- Personal observations on site > • continuous reassessment en route

1 Snow and Weather Conditions
- How much new snow has fallen on the slope you are going to ride?
- Recent wind deposition?
- Influence of solar radiation?
- Where could a slab release?
- How big would the slab be?

2 Terrain
- Situation (terrain and people) above and below
- Steepest section: how steep?
- Aspect?
- Typical avalanche terrain: steep, rocky slope; steep leeward slope; steep shaded forest glade?
- Slope shape
- Elevation
- Frequent traffic (regularly tracked-out slope)

3 Human Factor
- Ability, discipline, fatigue of group members
- Precautions:
> Safety distance
> Go one at a time
> Follow same track
> Identify "islands of "safety" as meeting points
- Avoid dangerous areas
- Avoid too risky routes
>> choose alternative routes

: decision

- Last check: to go ... or not to go

 > > check your line!

When you try to assess possible dangers, there is always a remaining risk due to the possibility of error. By looking at the three relevant factors that create avalanche danger, you are able to reduce the risk of error and thereby also the risk of an accident.

"The 3x3 Filter Method is like a three-layer safety net with three large to fine mesh nets on top of each other." (Werner Munter)

> > **It is up to you whether you play Russian roulette (consciously or unconsciously) or take responsibility for your own risk management by using the 3x3 Filter Method.**

Before you ride onto a slope, you have to ask yourself (3x3=9x) whether or not it is safe. The starting point is always the regional assessment. If you reach the decision that snow conditions, terrain and the makeup of your group are suitable for a day of true adventure, you can pack your gear and set off.

> > **Before you approach a certain slope, check the entire terrain carefully. If everything seems okay locally, you may go ahead.**

Before you actually get onto the slope, you have to answer the three questions one more time on the spot. If the answer is yes three times, you should be relatively safe. Always follow that order from the wider area to the region to the defined spot or you may fall through the tightest safety net at the beginning of the procedure. Again: the regional assessment (in the preparation phase) is followed by the evaluation of local dangers. Only then may you proceed to the zonal assessment that filters out the largest part of potential risks and serves as a final safety check of all decisions made up to that point.

> > **If the answer is no just once, you must not proceed.**

If you ignore that one "no," the filter method does not work and the safety net is ineffective.

We tend to overlook danger clues and focus more on signs of safety. In mountain regions, you will nearly always find danger indicators as well as signs of safe conditions. All you need is awareness and objectivity.

> > **The difficulty lies in recognizing all information provided by the snowpack, weather and terrain and processing it correctly.**

The 3x3 Filter Method is quick and easy to learn. Applying the method in the field doesn't take much time either. If you are willing to check the avalanche bulletin every time before you set off and keep your eyes and ears open while you are on the slope, this method will be 99 percent safe.

However, 99 percent safety means one percent remaining risk of triggering a slide. This one percent may cost you your life! But there are other methods that can help reduce risks. Werner Munter also developed the Reduction Method, which is fun to use together with the 3x3 Filters and offers a high degree of safety.

: The Reduction Method –

Decision Making in Critical Situations

☎Andi Schwarz △ Zugspitze, Germany ⚲Holger Feist, René Margreiter

A New Approach to Avalanche Safety

The Reduction Method was developed after a series of terrible avalanche accidents had shown that methods existing at that time were insufficient to reliably assess danger on individual slopes. The remaining risk was simply too high. For a long time it was assumed that the results obtained from glide block tests and other methods of examining snowpack stability would also apply to other slopes in the immediate surroundings, as long as they shared the same aspect, inclination and elevation. That was a fatal error!

> "The snowpack is characterized by its irregular structure."

It was precisely that error that was ultimately responsible for terrible accidents. Observations show that even after snow-slab release, some areas of the snowpack often remain intact. If you choose such an island of safety within an ocean of instability for a rutschblock test or snow pit and apply the results to other slopes, you might as well take dancing lessons in a minefield. No one standing in a minefield would ever assume that a similar looking spot was safe just because no mine has exploded on the spot where he or she is standing.

Unfortunately, the snowpack's stability can vary extremely within only a few yards. If you want to make "very safe" decisions by using the "classical" approach to avalanche safety, you'll spend more time on stability tests than on riding or skiing. Assessing avalanche danger always starts with determining a slope's inclination, since in the end it is always a slope's steepness that causes the snow to slide. To reliably estimate slope angle, you'll need some experience. If you practice regularly and check with an inclinometer, you'll soon become surprisingly accurate in judging slope angle. The fact that you'll tend to estimate slope angle higher than it really is provides for a certain safety margin.

Here are some clues to help you determine slope angle (see also Chapter 1):

> **Steep rocky slopes,**
> **Slopes with evidence of loose snow slides, and**
> **The inside (glacier side) of moraines...**
... are steeper than 39 degrees.

Again:
> Any slope that is steep enough to provide good riding in deep powder is avalanche terrain.

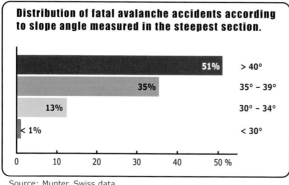

Distribution of fatal avalanche accidents according to slope angle measured in the steepest section.

51%	> 40°
35%	35° – 39°
13%	30° – 34°
< 1%	< 30°

The steeper the run, the better the fun... and the higher the risk!

Source: Munter, Swiss data

:The Reduction Method for Beginners

This straightforward method can be summarized in one basic rule that could help avoid around 75 percent of all avalanche accidents, if everybody observed it.

At Moderate danger, stay on slopes flatter than 40 degrees; at Considerable Danger, stay on slopes flatter than 35 degrees; and at High Danger, stay on flat terrain with an inclination of less than 30 degrees (or spend the day at a ski area on controlled trails).

The Reduction Method offers you more flexibility and freedom of movement. In Europe it is already widespread and successfully used and taught in avalanche courses.

:Decision Making: To go … or not to go

No one can ever be 100 percent sure whether skiing a certain slope will trigger an avalanche. Only after an accident occurs, when it is obviously too late, is it possible to find out why it happened. This is the great dilemma of evaluating avalanche danger. Freeskiers and riders always have to estimate potential danger, and every estimate involves a margin for error. Not every source (e.g., weak spot) of danger within the terrain is recognizable; some are completely hidden. There is always a remaining risk of triggering a slide. If you don't care about safety measures in the backcountry, you won't live long. If you want 100 percent safety, you have to stay at home. The solution lies in finding an acceptable limit. This acceptable limit was set to equal that of a summer hike in the mountains. Such a low remaining risk would drastically reduce the number of avalanche victims and still offer reasonable freedom of movement for individual freeriders. A method can be successful only if it is widely used and accepted. A method that requires you to stay at home at the slightest danger would soon loose its credibility. Certainly the number of deadly road accidents could be reduced to a minimum by enforcing a speed limit of 35 miles per hour. But even if such a system could save a great number of lives, it would never work. Anybody who drives a car accepts a certain risk on every ride!

The Reduction Method aims at estimating the overall risk and then reducing it to the lowest possible remaining risk by adopting a suitable code of conduct. Hence the name **Reduction Method**. Based on probability theory and statistical data collected over many years, Werner Munter developed the following formula for calculating avalanche risk:

$$\text{Risk} = \frac{\text{nature}}{\text{humans}} = \frac{\text{conditions}}{\text{conduct}} = \frac{\text{danger potential}}{\text{safety measures}}$$

Formula for acceptable remaining risk:

$$\text{Acceptable remaining risk} = \frac{\text{danger potential}}{\text{safety measure} \quad \text{X} \quad \text{safety measure}} \leq 1^\circ$$

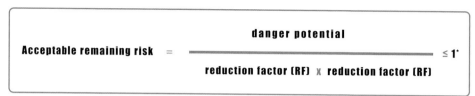

Acceptable remaining risk $= \dfrac{\text{danger potential}}{\text{reduction factor (RF)} \times \text{reduction factor (RF)}} \leq 1^*$

*The value one is the limit of acceptable remaining risk. The risk level in mountain environments can never be reduced to zero. It is up to you whether you choose to ignore that limit and take a greater risk, for instance level 1.33. The Reduction Method provides you with a clear guideline: You know how much risk you take.

The Reduction Method provides mountain guides, freeriders and ski mountaineers with a standard procedure for quick decision making. The result will either be a clear yes or a clear no, in other words "to go ... or not to go." Avalanche danger is no longer assessed on the basis of countless variables, such as static friction or shear stress, but on the basis of known constants such as slope inclination, terrain features and information from maps.

Information on general avalanche danger level and snowpack composition is provided by the avalanche bulletin. This information is readily available for everybody, and with some practice it is easy to understand.

The higher the danger level stated in the AB, the higher the danger potential of a given area. The Reduction Method assigns a corresponding danger potential to each danger level. These danger potentials describe the total of all risks to be expected in a given area. The higher the danger potential, the higher the probability of triggering a slide. Research on snowpack stability has shown that the danger potential (the total of all dangerous spots) doubles as danger rises one level:

> **Low Danger**   =   danger potential 2
> **Moderate Danger**   =   danger potential 4
> **Considerable Danger**   =   danger potential 8
> **High Danger**   =   danger potential 16 and higher

Hazard levels of the avalanche bulletin

For your independent assessment you may use any value in between these steps. For instance, if the AB states **Moderate Danger** (with a value of four) but your own observations indicate that danger could be higher, you should choose a value of six for **Moderate** to **Considerable** danger.

Safety measures are risk-reduction factors (RF). If you adopt several safety measures, multiply RF value for each of them to calculate the remaining risk. The product must be equal to or larger than the danger potential (the risk of triggering an avalanche) or else these measures are not effective.

Reduction factors belong to one of the three classes listed below, depending on their importance for preventing an avalanche accident.

> Slope angle — first-class factor
> Aspect and previous tracks — second-class factor
> Group size and safety distance for stress relief — third-class factor

Reduction Factors (RF) = Safety Measures

No. 1 or	Steepest slope section 35°–39° (less than 40°)	RF value: 2 first-class
No. 2 or	Steepest slope section around 35°	RF value: 3 first-class
No. 3	Steepest slope section 30°–34° (less than 35°)	RF value: 4 first-class

A first-class factor is required at Considerable Danger!

No. 4 or	Avoid the north sector: (northwest to north-northeast aspects)	RF value: 2 second-class
No. 5 or	Avoid the "northern half" of the compass (as shown below): west-northwest to east-southeast aspects	RF value: 3 second-class
No. 6	Avoid critical aspects and elevations as defined in the current avalanche bulletin	RF value: 4 second-class
No. 7	Use regularly tracked-out (highly frequented) slopes	RF value: 2 second-class

All second-class reduction factors are invalid with wet snow conditions!

> See also Points 2 and 3 of the "Important Notes" listed on the next page.

No. 8 or	Large group (more than 4 members) keeping a safe distance apart	RF value: 2 third-class
No. 9 or	Small group (2–4 members)	RF value: 2 third-class
No.10	Small group keeping a safe distance apart	RF value: 3 third-class

The minimum safe distance when ascending is 30 feet (10 meters). A very large distance is required when descending.

The aspect sectors of the Reduction Method:

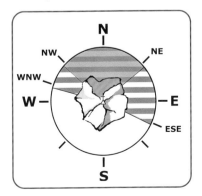

Sector North

Sector North includes northwest-north-northeast – if you avoid these aspects >> use Reduction Factor 2.

Sector Northern Half

Sector Northern Half includes west-northwest to east-southeast – if you avoid these aspects >> use Reduction Factor 3.

Important Notes:

> At **Considerable** danger, you must stay clear of steep rocky slopes, as these are steeper than 39 degrees inclination. Avoid jumps off cliffs and cornices.

> If the avalanche bulletin declares **all** aspects as dangerous, then reduction factors No. 4 to 7 are invalid. This is often the case when the critical amount of new snow is exceeded or when the snowpack is wet.

> Inverse conditions: Are south aspects more dangerous than north aspects? If the avalanche bulletin declares that south-facing slopes are more dangerous than north-facing slopes, or if there is any other evidence for such a situation, reduction factors 4 and 5 become invalid!

> At **High** Danger you must remain in moderately steep terrain (an inclination of less than 30 degrees).

> Inclination is always measured at a slope's **steepest section**, not where you happen to be at the moment.

> The Reduction Method is not applicable for snowmobilers. The additional loads their heavy vehicles put on the snowpack are simply too high.

Werner Munter says:

"The Reduction Method allows a quick assessment of individual slopes (10 to 30 seconds) that includes the following risk factors:

> Danger potential
> Slope inclination (steepest section)
> Aspect
> Size of group
> Safety measures (safe distance, etc.)
> How frequently a slope is ridden or skied.

> > This risk check tells you how likely a given combination of factors is to produce an accident, compared with accidents that happened in the past."

More information about using the Reduction Method

> Always apply the danger potential of the most unfavorable aspect. If, for instance, danger is Moderate for south slopes and Considerable for north slopes, assume a danger potential of 8.

> Highly frequented slopes include popular freeride slopes (often accessible from ski lifts), out-of-bounds areas, popular tours and backcountry classics. To qualify as highly frequented, a slope (including the starting zones of potential slides) must be tracked regularly after each snowfall.

> Channels, depressions and funnel-like terrain features always have several aspects. A channel's sidewalls are often steeper than its longitudinal axis.

> When you measure a slope's inclination on the map, observe that many slopes have an S-shaped profile with a steeper middle section. If you measure such a slope's inclination, you will only get an approximate average slope angle. Don't forget that some slope sections will always be considerably steeper than what you can see on the map.

> If you know an area thoroughly, this knowledge can be incorporated in the 3x3 Filter Method.

> **Warning:** The Reduction Method does not take into consideration a slope's size, elevation, proximity to ridges, and any other terrain features and peculiarities! Include your own observations when using the 3x3 Filter Method.

Where can the Reduction Method be used?

The Reduction Method works best for the Northern Hemisphere in the region between 40 degrees and 50 degrees latitude. It is almost as reliable in the region between 35 degrees and 40 degrees as well as between 50 degrees and 55 degrees latitude. In other words it works for the European Alps and the most popular ski areas in the United States and Canada.

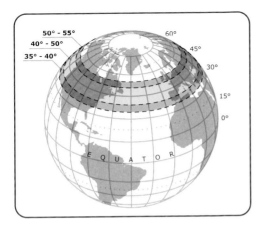

The Reduction Method can be used anywhere between 40° and 50° northern latitude. Further south, in the area between 35° and 40° latitude, solar radiation is stronger and snowpacks are usually more stable. This creates an extra safety margin for the Reduction Method. Between 50° and 55° northern latitude, the Reduction Method can also be used, but the method might be less reliable in these areas.

The best working way to assess the avalanche danger level is to use the 3x3 Filter Method complemented by intuition and observation and double-checked with the Reduction Method.

⌖Andi Schwarz △ Turkey ⚐Claire Auer

> > Example of 3x3 Filter and Reduction Methods

Four freeriders are going on a tour in northern Colorado in late winter. The group consists of two skiers and two snowboarders.

The snowpack is fairly deep; at an elevation of 8,000 feet (2,439 meters), the snow depth is approximately eight feet (2.5 meters).

The avalanche bulletin indicates a Moderate danger. Dangerous areas are steep shady slopes and chutes of all aspects. These areas are filled with unstable wind slabs deposited during the last storm. The weather has been good for the past two days, sunny and with relatively mild temperatures.

After three hours the group has reached the highest elevation of the tour. At approximately 11,500 feet (3,500 meters) above sea level, they access an east-facing slope with an inclination of about 40 degrees.

> > Use of the 3x3 Filter Method:

1. **Coarse filter. Regional assessment — preparation before leaving home**

1/9 Conditions (snow and weather): The AB indicates a Moderate danger. The weather forecast is for good and stable weather; temperatures are expected to rise moderately. 30 degrees Fahrenheit at 6,500 feet (−1 degree Celsius at 2,000 meters) >> OK!

2/9 Terrain: The group has examined the slope on the map; its inclination appears to be 40 degrees ("should have some powder") >> should be possible.

3/9 Human factor: All group members know each other, all are trained in avalanche safety, carry suitable equipment and know how to use it. The group is not too large >> good preconditions.

> Result of regional assessment: Go ahead!

2. **Medium filter, Local assessment during ascent**

4/9 Conditions: Snow becomes increasingly dry and powdery but also wind-packed. Sastrugi and small ripples are visible on the snow surface. Weather is still good. >> hmm, still okay.

5/9 Terrain: Two group members have been here before. The ascent is on a 30-degree ridge. >> should be fine.

6/9 Human factor: No problem. The group has toured together on other occasions; no one has a tendency to take excessive risks. Transceivers were checked. >> Okay.

> The situation looks good; the group continues.

3. **Fine Filter. On-spot assessment — to go ... or not to go!**

7/9 Conditions: Below the peak there is a foot-thick layer of lightly wind-packed powder. Smaller evidence of wind loading on the snow surface. >> Well...?!

8/9 Terrain: The east slope is very open in its middle section and gets steeper. Estimated inclination 40 degrees minimum! >> Well...? That's perfect avalanche terrain!

9/9 Human factor: Everyone wants to make first tracks. Riders must go one at a time in this terrain. >> There are reasons for doubt.

Low risk, high fun!

⊡ Stephan Boegli ⚐ Seb Michaud

10 — Decision making in the group

Three freeriders want to take a chance; one is unsure. Remain objective. Don't play down the risk; don't talk yourself into it ("it'll be alright...").

In critical situations you should use the Reduction Method, as it forces you to face the existing risk even though the most tempting run of the entire season may be at stake.

Assessment and decision by Reduction Method

Risk: Moderate danger level = danger potential 4

> Slope: greater than 40 degrees (steepest section) >> no first-class reduction factor (safety measure) is possible
> Aspect: East >> second-class RF value of 2, as riding won't be in the northern sector.
> Group: Four experienced riders/skiers = small group >> third-class RF value of 2 (or 3, if riders go one at a time).

> $$\frac{4}{2 \times 3} = \text{remaining risk } 0.667$$

Result: acceptable remaining risk.

From a statistical point of view, the risk of riding that slope is not higher than that of a summer hike in the mountains. If there are no further objections (evidence of recent avalanching or other danger indicators), the group may go ahead. No need to mention the need of picking a smart line that avoids danger spots.

Know your line!

If you stick to the Reduction Method, you will sometimes avoid a slope that is ridden by some reckless adrenaline freaks. That can be hard to take. In return, the Reduction Method will probably reward you with many years of riding and skiing, and that's what matters.

Freeriders with limited experience should start off by using the Reduction Method for Beginners and become familiar as soon as possible with the 3x3 Filter Method and the Reduction Method. With a little practice, they'll quickly learn these methods.

Nonetheless, it is highly recommended that all beginners take a practical avalanche course or participate in a freeride camp to acquire the necessary basic skills (see Chapter 8).

"Sometimes it's so good that you just don't care if you die. And here is where things get euphoria runs rampant on sunny days with fresh powder in large, tempting slopes. Always be suspicious of this combination."

Bruce Tremper, Avalanche Expert

Richard Walch

:Setting a Risk Limit to Avoid Catastrophic Accidents

During the winter of 1999–2000, several terrible avalanche accidents happened in Austria. In early winter, nine individuals died on a guided tour with certified mountain guides. In late winter, 12 skiers were killed by another avalanche. Both accidents had one thing in common: The individuals involved were not careless greenhorns but experienced mountaineers and mountain guides.

These examples showed yet another time that avalanches don't care about their victim's level of knowledge, and that even experts are killed by snow slides.

An investigation of statistical data revealed a **risk limit** beyond which the risk of an avalanche accident rises drastically. Using the **Limit Strategy** based on this data, you can make sure you won't exceed the absolute maximum acceptable risk!

Every freerider knows the dangerous spiral of the white rush. One ride is better than the one before, and the last one tops them all. The Limit Strategy was developed to keep your dream from turning into a nightmare.

> > When you are caught in the white rush, the Limit Strategy can protect you from yourself.

One ride is better than the one before and the last one tops them all.

Inspired by Jan Mersch, 2001

It is up to you to decide how much risk you want to take. Caught in the white rush and competing with their companions for the best lines, many riders "forget" to use the Reduction Method (or other viable systems of risk management). Be wary when thoughts like "it'll be alright" appear. Don't stop using your head. Even if you heed no other warning, never ignore the Limit. You break that rule at your own risk.

The Limit Strategy

> At **Moderate** danger:

In rarely frequented, shady slopes (those with northwest, north or northeast aspects), stay away from inclinations of more than 39 degrees.

> At **Considerable** danger:

Stay away from slopes steeper than 39 degrees regardless of their aspects! This rule does not apply to highly frequented freeride/freeski areas that are directly accessible from ski lifts without further hiking or traversing or that are subject to avalanche-control measures.

PowderGuide Tip

For shady freeride slopes with northwest, north or northeast aspects in areas accessible from ski lifts but not subjected to avalanche-control measures, 39 degrees is a reasonable limit. In other aspects, check your risk and make a responsible decision. Accidents do happen in other aspects! The risk is **high**, and less may be more!

> At **High** danger:

Stay away from slopes 30 degrees or steeper. Warning: Avalanches may advance very far onto flat terrain.

A slab avalanche triggered by a skier. Above the Limit?   ☏ **Bavarian Avalanche Warning Service.**

> > **Warning:**

The Limit defines the maximum risk that European mountain guides should not exceed when they guide tours in the backcountry. Remember that their high degree of experience and snow-how enables them to find good routes even in critical situations. For regular freeriders, who are much less experienced, the Limit is the limit — without any exception!

The hike is more than worth it. The first descent at "Cuemmel's Peak."

⊕John Speer △ Kodiak Island, Alaska ⚲Markus "Cuemmel" Grünfelder

> The 3x3 Filter Method, the Reduction Method and the Limit Strategy were developed for responsible freeriders and freeskiers who want to apply methods of risk management that help them to get safely through the winter season. These methods are not a free ticket for adrenaline freaks. No method can ever be 100 percent safe. Only you can decide how much risk you want to take.

Since these principles of risk management were introduced to avalanche safety some years ago, a number of similar methods emerged. We recommend that all freeriders use the 3x3 Filter Method in combination with the Reduction Method. This system allows for a high degree of flexibility without neglecting the need for clear limits.

Again, no method can ever be 100 percent safe. "To go … or not to go," the decision is yours. But no matter which method you use, the Limit must always be the absolute limit. If you go beyond the Limit, you are dancing in a minefield.

:What to Do If No Recent Avalanche Bulletin is Available

In many areas of North America, avalanche bulletins are unavailable or only published on an irregular basis. What should you do in such cases? Can the Reduction Method still be applied? Or should you go back to digging snow pits and doing rutschblock tests for hours on end?

The answer is easier than you may think: Just make your own avalanche forecast, and then apply the Reduction Method as usual. How to do that? By observing clues and recognizing potential dangers that arise from the various factors that create avalanches (snow, wind, sun, temperature, terrain).

1. **Is there a critical amount of new snow? (See page 43)**
2. **Are there any alarm signs?**
3. **Are there any clues (such as ripples or dunes, sastrugi, new cornices) on the snow surface that indicate recent wind loading?**
4. **The weather:**
> How much time has passed since the last snowfall?
> How much did it snow?
> How intense is the solar radiation (taking seasonal peculiarities into account)? Has the sun favored settlement or has it destabilized the snowpack by thawing it to a dangerous degree?
> What were the temperature patterns over the past few days and previous night, and what's expected for the next day?
> Was there any dangerous wind loading? What about wind activity at high altitudes?

You may be able to get an avalanche bulletin for an area close by that provides at least some useful information for your own prognosis. A regional weather report may also be helpful.

In order to play safe and avoid potentially deadly mistakes, you should start at the highest danger level and downgrade your evaluation step by step if any mitigating factors are present.

Each danger level has its own characteristics and clues that help you make a fairly accurate evaluation of actual danger.

Procedure for Assessing Avalanche Danger

The highest danger level, Extreme Danger **(Level 5)**, can usually be excluded from the beginning. At Extreme Danger, roads and settlements exposed to avalanche danger are no longer accessible, and the danger potential is so high that large and very large avalanches will likely occur in all areas. There are no safe slopes or areas. Extreme Danger usually lasts only a short period. This danger level is rarely declared, and occurs only after extremely strong snowfalls.

High Danger **(Level 4)** is also relatively uncommon and declared only on a few days in winter. At High danger, unstable snowpack can be found in all aspects. The following warning signs indicate High danger and **very dangerous** conditions for freeriding:

> The amount of new snow exceeds the critical level.
> Natural avalanches are large and penetrate far into flat terrain.
> Remote triggering over large distances is common.
> Further alarm signs such as cracks shooting through the snowpack, whumpfing sounds and evidence of recent avalanche activity are common.

Considerable Danger (Level 3) is the **critical situation** for freeriders. Even though the danger is less obvious than at High or Extreme danger or even completely hidden, the snowpack is only moderately stable or is unstable on many slopes. Indicators of Considerable danger include the following:

> The critical amount of new snow has been reached.
> New snow was deposited in windy conditions and /or at low temperatures.
> New snow fell on a snowpack that was subjected to faceting (sugar snow) or on a layer of ice or very old snow. New snow on top of surface hoar is even worse!
> **Warning!** In particularly adverse conditions (such as wind deposition of loose snow at low temperatures), the danger level may reach Considerable without any new snow.
> The snowpack becomes water-saturated and cannot support your weight, sending you postholing.
> Frequent **whumpfing** can be heard.
> Natural avalanches are common in steep and rocky terrain.
> An individual rider may easily trigger a slide in steep terrain.
> Remote triggering from the bottom of a slope may be possible.

Moderate Danger (Level 2) is the **normal** level of snowpack stability. The snowpack is unstable on some steep slopes. Indicators of Moderate danger include the following:

> No indicators of Considerable or High danger.
> Avalanches can be triggered on unstable slopes with high additional loads.
> Avalanches may be triggered by single persons on very unstable slopes, and even natural avalanches are occasionally possible.
> Natural avalanches are usually small (except in springtime).

Low Danger (Level 1) is also a common level. At Low danger the snowpack is generally well settled and internal stresses are very low. Avalanche activity is limited to sluffs, particularly when the snow is wet. The situation is very favorable. Nevertheless, slab avalanches may be triggered by large groups and other high additional loads in extreme terrain. Indicators of Low danger include:

> No danger indicators or alarm signs.
> In spring the snowpack is completely covered in a melt-freeze crust in the morning after clear nights. (Danger may increase during the day with rising temperatures.)
> The snowpack is deep and well settled, and consists of fine-grained old snow. (The most important factor is bonding between individual layers. Since bonding and the absence of weak layers are hard to evaluate and vary widely in each individual type of snowpack, only highly experienced snow scientists with detailed knowledge of weather patterns throughout the winter are able to make such assessments.)

Level 5

Extreme Avalanche Hazard: numerous large avalanches produced by natural release. Catastrophic situation!
Freeriding? No Way!
☞Tyrolean Avalanche Warning Service

Level 4

Avalanches may advance into flat terrain, particularly at High danger levels. Observe runout zones!
☞Bavarian Avalanche Warning System

Level 3

Considerable Hazard: Massive wind loading (with or without newly fallen snow) creates dangerous snow slabs.
☞Thorsten Indra

Level 2

Moderate Hazard: Dangerous spots are clearly visible. Wind direction from left to right. Snow was removed from the ridges and deposited in gullies. Time since deposition favored stabilization of windblown snow.
☞Helmut Mittermayr

Level 1

Low Hazard – but still a lot of fun.
A solid crust has formed overnight. Increasing solar radiation during the day softens this crust into spring snow.
☞Thorsten Indra

Time is an important factor in the development of danger. After a snowfall, the danger level generally recedes over time, but the following factors must be considered:

> The absence of further (significant) wind deposition indicates stabilization.
> With large amounts of new snow, settlement tends to occur faster due to the high weight.
> The danger remains high after a dump for a minimum of approximately two to three days.
> Sunny slopes usually settle faster and show lower internal stresses than shady slopes.
> Mild temperatures around the freezing point reduce the danger more quickly than constantly low temperatures (colder than 18 degrees Fahrenheit, or -8 degrees Celsius).
> The danger can remain high for several weeks if new snow falls on surface hoar (a persistent weak layer).

Warning: The absence of danger indicators is unfortunately not always a guarantee for good, stable conditions (Low or Moderate danger). The danger is often hidden. **This is typical of Considerable danger, which is why this level is so dangerous and prone to produce accidents.**

In early and mid winter, the avalanche danger level often increases with rising altitude, so that level may be Moderate at an elevation of 6,500 feet (2,000 meters) but Considerable at 10,000 feet (3,000 meters). In spring, however, the situation may be safer at high altitudes than farther down, where temperatures are generally higher and cause dangerous thawing of the snowpack.

> **In order to avoid deadly mistakes in evaluating avalanche danger, you should always start with an overly cautious assessment. Only if clear indicators of positive factors are present should you scale down your evaluation to the next lower level.**

The better you know a given area and its weather patterns throughout the winter, the better you'll be at evaluating the situation.

You'll find that your assessment becomes more accurate the more time you spend in a given area. Avalanches don't always stick to the rules, which is why you must never rely on a single factor. Try to incorporate all available information and danger indicators to reduce the risk of overlooking a decisive factor.

If you put all the pieces of information together like a jigsaw puzzle, your prognosis will be built on a solid base of evidence. Provided that you interpret the facts correctly, your assessment should be very accurate.

A defensive strategy is always advisable for freeriders, at least for those who want to grow old in the mountains. If no avalanche bulletin is available, you lack the most important piece of information for your independent risk check. Without an AB you must be even more defensive and continually question your own evaluation. Part of such a strategy is to be a watchdog and always keep your eyes and ears open for possible danger indicators. If you suspect that your initial assessment was too optimistic, step up the danger level. It's your life that's at stake! The same is true for evaluation by a group. As long as there is no unanimous decision, assume that the most pessimistic evaluation is correct.

Snow Profiles and Shear Tests

Digging snow pits and performing shear tests allow you to check the potential for avalanches on a particular spot of a given area. There are several problems with these tests:

> A single snow pit or rutschblock does not provide sufficient information for assessing avalanche danger in other (even similar) slopes. In order to reliably evaluate the danger, you would have to do 10 to 12 snow pits and/or rutschblocks, and then it would be time to go back home!

> Proper interpretation of snow pits requires a lot of experience, which is why it makes sense only for experts to dig them.

> This doesn't mean that taking a closer look at a snowpack's structure is worthless. Digging can provide you with very interesting insights into the nature of snow. But it is simply unrealistic and dangerous to try assessing avalanche danger on the basis of only a few local shear tests (see p. 38 about hot spots and the irregular structure of the snowpack).

Warning! In situations that require you to make your own avalanche forecast, always stick to the following two-step procedure:

> Assess the avalanche danger level (judge the potential for avalanches).

> Make a decision on whether or not to ride a slope.

It is vital to keep these two steps separate. If you mix up the process of gathering information with that of making a decision, you will be tempted to cheat on yourself. Just like anybody else, freeriders tend to see only what they want to see, particularly when they're caught up in the white rush!

>> Chapter 4. Backcountry Equipment

☞Jancsi Hadik 🛇Nicolas Falquet

The right equipment is indispensable for freeriding. In the worst case, your life can depend on it. But the best equipment is worthless if you don't know how to use it properly. In a ski area, you can always count on the ski patrol if you are in an accident. In the backcountry, you depend solely on yourself and your companions for help.

This chapter gives an overview of necessary freeride and freeskiing equipment and the latest innovations and products available on the market. However, this information cannot replace practical experience in handling this equipment. Since you are exposed to avalanche hazard in the backcountry, you need the following items in addition to your basic gear (a snowboard or skis, boots, bindings and functional clothing).

The basic safety equipment for anyone who likes to ride powder snow consists of:
> Avalanche beacon or transceiver
> Daypack
> Avalanche shovel
> Avalanche probe

For open terrain you also need:
> Compass (with adjustable declination)
> Clinometer (standalone or integrated with a compass)
> Map (largest available scale)
> First-aid kit
> Watch
> Emergency food (e.g., energy bars)
> (Thermos)

Other useful items include:
> Altimeter
> Helmet
> Back protector
> Cell phone
> GPS (global positioning system)
> Headlamp (LED lamp)
> Thermometer

In remote areas where you can't return to patrolled trails within a short time, you have to rely even more on yourself. You should add the following items to your standard equipment:
> Bivouac sack
> Food and drink
> Tools and repair kit

Additional equipment:
> Avalanche Airbag System
> Avalung
> Avalanche Ball
> Recco System

Snowboard, telemark skis, alpine skis or snowshoes

Snowboard, telemark skis, alpine skis or simply snowshoes — there are many ways of enjoying the magic of winter. Every person who goes into the backcountry has his or her own preferences, and that's just fine. That's why in this chapter we will focus on those items that are essential for all freeriders and freeskiers. We would also like to introduce some new and innovative products, such as collapsible ascent skis and split boards.

The most important thing when choosing your gear is getting the best quality you can afford — gear that is absolutely reliable. There is nothing worse than having to walk down the hill after a strenuous uphill hike because of a broken binding or having your fun factor reduced by half in a one-legged ride. For backcountry touring in particular, it is important that you regularly check and maintain your gear, to ensure that it is always in perfect condition.

Clothing

Good-quality functional clothing is highly recommended for the backcountry. Modern high-tech fibers transport moisture away from your skin and outperform conventional cotton. High-tech material will soon feel dry after a strenuous ascent, while cotton would keep you soaked in cold sweat for the rest of the day. Functional clothing reduces the risk of catching a cold (or hypothermia in the worst case) and increases comfort. It makes sense to start with a layer of functional underwear and add one or more layers for insulation according to temperature. Layering enables you to adapt perfectly to changing weather conditions. The outer layer naturally consists of wind- and water-proof jacket and pants.

Avalanche Beacons or Transceivers

Just as you would never leave your house without putting on some clothes, you should never venture into the backcountry without your transceiver! If you are buried in an avalanche and carry a transceiver, you can be located by anyone who is equipped with a similar device and knows how to use it. Modern transceivers are always transmitters as well as receivers, hence the name. When your beacon is set on transmitting while you are skiing, it emits a signal that humans can't hear. If someone is buried in a slide, you simply switch your beacon to receive the signal from the buried person. That way you are able to track the signal and hopefully locate the victim, if you are trained and understand how to do a search.

Avalanche transceivers

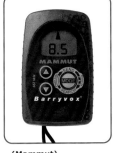  

(Mammut)   (Tracker)   (Ortovox)

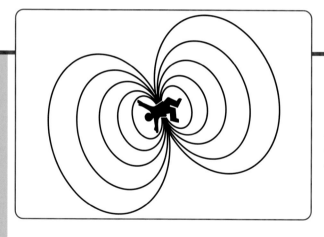

The induction lines emitted by the transceiver guide the search team to the buried person. When switched on receiving, the beacon is used to track these lines. Due to the curved shape of the induction lines, a special search technique is used that requires some practice.

How Transceivers Work

Similar to a magnet, the transceiver creates an electromagnetic field. It does this by emitting an electromagnetic signal at a standardized frequency of 457 kHz (kilohertz). Due to the curved shape of these induction lines, the signal does not lead you to the buried person in a straight line. Instead, a special searching method is required. The effective range of a beacon depends on the position of the transmitter's antenna in relation to that of the receiver and typically lies between 20 and 80 yards (meters and yards are about the same). All modern transceivers currently available on the market use the same standardized frequency and are therefore fully compatible. These little life-savers have to endure temperatures between –22 degrees and 104 degrees Fahrenheit (–30 degrees and 40 degrees Celsius). The energy consumption must be low enough to keep the device working in an avalanche for a period of eight days. One set of batteries lasts for a minimum of 20 days in the backcountry. Rechargeable batteries are unsuitable, as they quickly lose capacity at low temperatures.

Digital or Analog System?

There are two transceiver systems on the market — digital and analog. Both types of transceivers produced by leading manufacturers are effective and reliable, but some models are a little easier to operate than others.

Analog Transceivers

Most older models belong to this type of transceiver. Analog units are generally very reliable, though they do not match the user-friendly handling of digital models. With some practice, it is possible to use analog transceivers very effectively.

The searching person follows an acoustic signal. Some models offer visual guidance via LEDs, which can be helpful when background noises are strong (e.g., in a storm). For the same reason, all analog models can be used with earphones. In order to locate the victim, the searcher moves in the direction of the loudest signal. The closer the buried person, the stronger the signal gets. When the loudest sound is heard, the volume is turned down and the signal becomes lower. This procedure is repeated until the minimum level is reached for the closest distance. Now the searcher proceeds to pinpoint the victim (see Chapter 5).

Digital Transceivers

Digital models are equipped with a visual display. They direct the searching person along the induction lines and continually compute the direction and distance of the buried person. Many models offer advanced functions, such as multiple burial search. Digital transceivers are generally easier to operate for less-experienced persons. Some transceivers, such as the Barryvox, allow the person searching to switch between digital and analog search mode. Try using a few different models before you make up your mind on which type you want to buy.

How to Use a Transceiver

The right time to check your transceiver's function is either at home in the morning, before you get on the ski lift or at the trailhead. Check each transceiver in the group for both functions — transmitting and receiving. If you should discover that a beacon is not fully functioning, there is still time to replace it. Wear your transceiver on your body; do not carry it in your pack or in the pocket of your jacket. Make sure that it is switched on! Many tragic accidents have involved people who carried a transceiver but could not be located because it wasn't transmitting. Check its function during every break.

Some models have harness systems with locking mechanisms that automatically switch on the transceiver as you put the harness on. Before you buy a transceiver, find out about the manufacturer's service and warranty policy. You should be able to have your beacon periodically checked at a service center, particularly after a fall that may have caused internal damage. Sometimes a beacon makes a rattling noise when you shake it. The noise may be caused by a broken antenna, which, at the least, reduces the beacon's effective range.

: Avalanche Shovel

If you think that you won't need a shovel because a snowboard is just as good for digging, just try it out in avalanche snow. It simply doesn't work!

A good avalanche shovel must meet a variety of criteria:

> Have an unbreakable blade and a sturdy handle
  (which is, unfortunately, not true for all models available on the market)
> Be lightweight and collapsible
> Have a good feel in your hands
> Have a large scoop
> Have no sharp edges that may cause injury in case of a fall
> Be suitable for digging kickers, emergency snow caves, snow pits
  (for examining snowpack composition) and more

Avalanche shovels by Black Diamond and Ortovox.

: Avalanche Probe

A collapsible avalanche probe belongs in every pack. It consists of a number of tubes that can be assembled into a long rod with a metal tip.

By pushing the probe into the snow, you can feel the presence of a buried object or person. A probe is a valuable tool for confirming the precise location of a victim after a beacon search and for determining the depth of burial. If you are looking for a person who does not carry a beacon, probing is the only way to begin the search before a professional rescue team arrives.

Additionally, an avalanche probe is also very useful for checking the landing zone of cliff jumps for hidden rocks.

Without a probe, you risk losing valuable time that may mean the difference between life and death.
(Avalanche probe by Mammut)

The indispensable minimum safety equipment for freeriding in the backcountry as well as on uncontrolled slopes around ski areas consists of a transceiver, an avalanche shovel and an avalanche probe.

In more remote areas that are not directly accessible from ski lifts, you also need the following equipment:

>: First-Aid Kit and Emergency Equipment

Important Notes:

> An emergency kit alone won't help you all by itself! Recent training is a must.
> Don't rely on one group member for first-aid skills and equipment. If this particular person is buried or injured, you are out of luck. For the same reason, the group should carry more than one first-aid kit for backup.
> The list of items on the following pages is only a general recommendation. Adapt this list to suit your personal needs, medical history and tour destination.
> Don't rely on prepacked first-aid kits, as they usually don't contain everything you may need. The selection of items is often based on profit rather than practical considerations. Quantity often seems more important than quality, and some items may even be useless (unsuitable bandages, scissors that don't work). Pack your own kit based on the selection of items shown on the following two pages.

Other Useful Items

> Duct tape is adhesive tape made of a very strong fabric. This versatile material provides excellent adhesion and has many uses, including first-aid (e.g., making a splint) or the emergency repair of broken gear. If you don't want to carry the whole roll, wrap a suitable length around a pencil.
> Nylon rope or cord (minimum length 30 feet, or 10 meters) for carrying, making a splint, repair work and more.

Bivouac Sack

A bivouac (bivy) sack is a small and lightweight emergency substitute for a tent. A bivy sack may help keep an injured person warm and protected from hypothermia. If you are caught in bad weather, a bivvy sack increases your chances of survival at low temperatures. In poor visibility, its bright colors may help attract the attention of rescuers. The absolute minimum equipment is an emergency bag made of heat-retaining foil.

Antiseptic ointment

Alcohol swab: For cleansing the area around a wound.

Sterile dressings (4 by 4's), compresses: Make sure they have a non-adherent coating. Do not use cotton or cellulose products.

Compeed plaster: Marketed in the United States as Band-Aid Advanced Healing Strips, this is a great product for preventing blisters. Adheres better if you apply tincture of benzoin (available in pharmacies and outdoor retailers).

Triangular bandages: Very versatile; may be worn as a scarf, used as a bandage or serve as a sling to immobilize an injured arm.

Large sterile dressing (burn dressing): To cover large wounds, such as compound fractures.

Elastic adhesive dressing: Used after surgery; easy to apply even on difficult spots.

Bandages with sterile dressings: Very useful two-in-one product. Make sure that dressings are non-adherent. Don't use conventional gauze rolls; they take up a lot of space and offer no advantage.

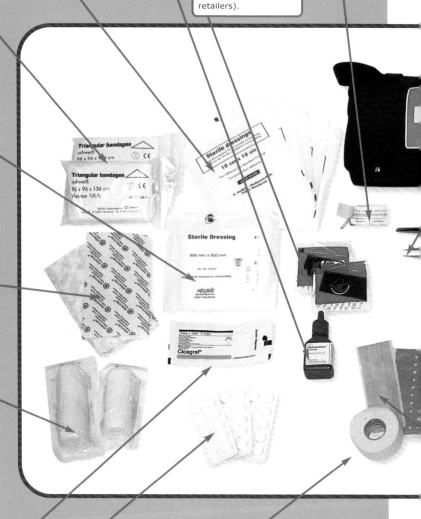

Consult your doctor about useful pharmaceutical products. For extended trips, you may need drugs prescribed by your doctor.

Plaster or sports tape: Effective for the prevention of blisters and other uses. Sports tape is more expensive but stronger, has better adhesion and is easy to tear off at the desired length.

Wound-closure strips: To close large, open wounds that would need stitching. Cleanse and disinfect the wound carefully before applying closure strips.

Tweezers:
Very versatile; use them to cleanse wounds, remove splinters, etc.

Dressing scissors:
It is worth spending some money on a pair of good scissors that can cut through clothing if necessary. One blade should have a sharp tip for lancing blisters, while the other tip should be blunt for safely cutting up bandages.

SAM Splint:
All-purpose splint, particularly suitable for immobilizing a foot, hand, lower arm and neck.

Elastic bandage:
A cohesive bandage is ideal. Individual layers adhere to each other and provide excellent support. "Vetwrap" is a cheap alternative available from vets or at pharmacies.

Emergency blanket:
Reflects body heat; water- and wind-proof; inexpensive.

Surgical gloves:
Protect against infection from body fluids.

Adhesive bandage strips:
For minor cuts. Don't buy a huge supply, as adhesion becomes very poor after one or two years in your kit.

CPR Microshield:
(manufactured by MDI): Protects against infection when performing mouth-to-mouth resuscitation.

CPR alternative:
Pocket rescue masks from Laerdal, Ambu or other manufacturers also prevent infection, though they are much larger than Microshields.

Clinometer

The clinometer is used to determine a slope's angle or steepness. In order to obtain a meaningful result, you should measure the angle of a section that is approximately as steep as the rest of the slope. For assessing avalanche hazard, always measure (or estimate) the steepest section.

The clinometer is used for determining slope angle. Note that the result is only accurate for the measured section!

Food and Drink

Appropriate caloric intake and proper hydration are preconditions for performance in sports. Apart from that, it is extremely important to carry some extra food for unexpected situations or for tours or rides that take longer than expected. In ski areas, you may rely on restaurants to keep you from starving and dehydrating. In the backcountry, where you have to provide for yourself, a candy bar can often taste like heaven. Therefore, always carry a generous ration of energy bars or other concentrated foods to supply vital energy in emergency situations.

Make sure that you also get enough to drink. At low winter temperatures, your body loses a lot of moisture through respiration. That moisture is visible in the cold air when your breath produces little clouds of steam. You may lose several quarts of water per day without even sweating.

Soda pop and beer may taste good but have a negative effect on endurance and performance. Apart from that, don't drink and ride! (You may find time for alcoholic refreshments in the evening.) Isotonic sports drinks are formulated to replenish lost fluids and minerals; they are available in powder form or ready to drink.

Tools and Repair Kit

Always bring a selection of tools and emergency-repair material for backcountry riding or longer trips. Some kits combine screwdrivers, pliers, scissors and other tools. A suitable length of duct tape, a few spare bolts and a piece of wire can save your day, as bindings tend to confirm Murphy's Law (what *can* go wrong, *will* go wrong) and break at the worst possible moment.

: Equipment for Touring

Skis / Telemark Skis / Approach Skis

Skis still remain the most effective ascent device. On backcountry snowboard tours, we were often overtaken by backcountry skiers even though they had started later than we did and seemed to move at a much more relaxed pace. A ski's sharp steel edges and skins offer great advantages in steep and icy terrain. Additionally, you can fit ski crampons on your bindings for very hard snow or extreme terrain.

> Special approach skis for snowboarders are now available on the market. For the do-it-yourself folks, there is always the alternative of cutting a pair of old skis in two and adding a detachable joint or a hinge of some sort in the middle. For the descent you can separate the two halves or fold up the skis and strap them to your backpack. Approach skis offer a variety of advantages over snowshoes, but their weight is considerably higher. Different models are available with bindings for soft boots, hard boots and step-in systems.

Snowshoes

Many snowboarders choose classic snowshoes for touring. Snowshoes come in a variety of different materials, shapes and constructions — all plastic, aluminum frame with synthetic decking, wood — at prices ranging from $100 to $350. Snowshoes fit all types of boots, including snowboard soft boots, and can be easily stowed inside or outside a backpack for the downhill ride. Don't buy snowshoes with lacing systems, as these tend to get loose. Look instead for ratchet buckles similar to those on soft boot bindings. Some models even feature step-in systems.

Snowshoes allow comfortably hiking on slopes below 30 degrees of inclination. When the terrain gets steeper, they tend to lose grip. Make sure to consider this fact when planning a trip.

Many modern snowshoes are equipped with very effective crampon-like claws. For a good grip, the claws at the pivot point should be supported by additional claws around the edges. Models that have only claws under the ball of the foot tend to rotate and slide, which reduces comfort and increases the risk of a fall in hard snow conditions.

Snowshoes (by Atlas)

Split boards

These touring snowboards can be split into a pair of ascent skis. The system combines the advantages of snowboarding for the descent (surf-style flotation) and of touring skis for the ascent and flat areas. Touring skis allow difficult ascents that are impossible on snowshoes. You will also travel much faster on skis. Though the first split boards could not quite match the performance of a true freeride board, there are now some good split boards on the market. Split boards also help save weight (important on long tours), since you don't have to carry your board uphill and descend with skis or snowshoes on your pack.

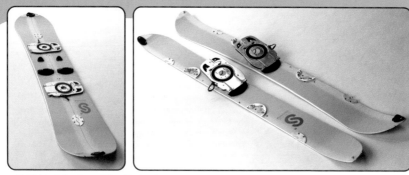

Split Decision board (by Burton)

Telescopic Poles

Telescopic poles are used together with snowshoes for better balance and stamina. Good poles are lightweight and collapsible for easy fastening onto the pack.

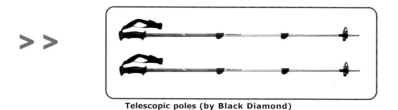

Telescopic poles (by Black Diamond)

Crampons and Piolets

When you hike with snowshoes in the spring, you are soon forced to put on crampons. On hard snow, trouble often starts at slope angles of 30 degrees. Terrain steeper than 35 degrees in icy conditions can become very dangerous. If you fall and start to slide, you quickly pick up speed and there is hardly any way to slow down and stop the fall. Therefore, make sure you put on your crampons early enough before conditions become critical.

Crampons for soft boots ... and for hard boots (by Mammut)   Ice axe (by Black Diamond)

Warning! Walking with crampons requires some practice. Without proper technique the front points may easily get caught in your trousers (not suitable for baggy pants!) or in the snow, if you don't lift your foot high enough.

> Note that crampons that can be used with soft boots are made for backcountry touring. Their bindings and the soft snowboard boots are not suitable for extreme conditions. For extra support and balance, use a light ice axe (piolet) — not to be confused with ice tools (axes) used for ice climbing.

Climbing Harness and Rope

For extreme tours and on glaciers, you need a climbing rope and harness to set up a rope team. If someone falls into a hidden crevasse, the rope stops the fall and the rest of the group can take up some of the fall's force and rescue that person. The rope can also be used to gain access to remote gullies and chutes or to get across difficult rocky sections. For effective use of a rope, you also need the following items:

> **Climbing harness**
> **Two screw-gate carabiners**
> **Five-mm cord**
> **Two Prusik slings**
> **Webbing**

Climbing harness and rope (by Mammut)

A rope provides a margin of safety only if you **learn** and **practice** how to use it properly. Amateur rope work can easily result in accidents. Consider hiring a qualified mountain guide for extreme tours and glacier travel.

Freeride Backpack

There are an endless variety of daypacks suitable for freeriding. Sizes range from 450 cubic inches (7 liters) to several thousand cubic inches (more than 50 liters), and a great variety of designs and harness systems are available. Remember: You don't recognize a good pack by its design. What matters is how well it works for you in the backcountry, and you can figure that out only by renting or borrowing several types of packs and testing them in the field.

One of the most important things about a pack is that it is comfortable to carry. The only way to test this is by packing it. The best thing to do is to stuff it with your gear. That way you can find out whether it all fits in comfortably.

A good pack must have durable seams and zips that work properly, even when the pack is full.

Other important features include:

> Hip and chest belts
> A separate compartment for the shovel blade
> Two compartments for stowing the shovel handle and the probe
> Room for a water bottle or hydration system (e.g., CamelBak)
> Straps for attaching ascent skis, poles and a piolet
> Solid carrying system for snowboard or skis

Freeride daypacks
(by Burton and Mammut)

The smallest type of backcountry packs are heli-packs with sizes ranging from 450 to 1,100 cubic inches. They are designed to hold only the most essential equipment. These packs are not suitable for long tours but are very useful and comfortable for out-of-bounds riding and heli boarding/skiing. A larger pack that holds between 1,350 and 1,850 cubic inches is recommended for half-day and day trips. This size provides enough extra space for food and drink, spare clothing and a fleece jacket. Packs larger than 2,150 cubic inches are available for longer tours of several days.

 >>

Freeride helmet (by Burton)

Helmet / Back Protector

Fortunately there are now more and more riders and skiers wearing helmets. While professional riders had been using them for a long time, many regular dudes thought that helmets were not compatible with their image. Snow-covered rocks, however, are hard to recognize. In case of a fall, it is only a matter of luck not to hit one, and any rock is harder than your skull. Special freeride helmets are available, and more and more riders will make a habit of using one. A helmet is a tremendous value for the money and particularly important in winters with shallow snowpacks, when rocks and stones are barely covered with snow, in the early season and throughout the year in rocky terrain. Keep in mind that the forces of a fall will always make your head hit the ground. Therefore, protect your gray matter!

>> Be smart — wear a helmet.

Again, we strongly recommend helmets for all freeriders who like to ride gullies, couloirs and steep rocky terrain. There is no better way to spend your money.

Another valuable piece of equipment comes from the world of motocross — a back protector. Some protectors are integrated in vests that are easy to put on and wear on top of a shirt. Together with your head, your spine is another extremely sensitive and important part of your body that is worth protecting.

Map / Compass / Altimeter

These three tools are very effective for orientation, if you know how to use them. Maps are indispensable not only for planning a tour, but also for finding the best route through terrain. Useful maps have a large scale; we recommend a scale of 1:24,000 (see Chapter 6).

The map allows you to identify terrain traps or dead-end routes and to determine the steepest sections and type of ground surface before you even leave home. Make sure that you are using recent maps, as even the backcountry changes. Little trees for instance, may grow over the years and become dense forests that pose unexpected nasty obstacles.

A compass is used for orientation and determining slope aspect (the compass direction of a slope's fall line). Some models have sighting mirrors that make it easier to take a bearing and some feature **integrated clinometers**. A compass is an inexpensive tool and offers good value for money (starting from $10). Make sure that you can adjust it for **declination**.

An altimeter reacts to changes in atmospheric pressure and displays the elevation of a given spot, which is important for orientation. Atmospheric pressure sinks with rising altitude. Since atmospheric pressure is influenced by meteorological conditions, you always have to set your altimeter to the known elevation of a point of reference before you set off and regularly calibrate it along the route (using other points of reference that you can find on the map). This characteristic may seem a disadvantage, but it can actually be helpful and warn you of a sudden change in weather while you are on your tour.

If, for instance, the altitude display increases even though you are not climbing any higher, this means that air pressure is falling and that weather conditions will probably get worse. An altimeter is very useful for orientation in poor visibility if you use it together with a map and compass. Unfortunately, altimeters tend to be rather expensive.

Mountaineering watch with compass, altimeter, weather forecaster and thermometer. (T-Touch by Tissot)

>> In uncertain weather conditions, stay on trails or in known terrain (unless you like to take substantial risks and have many years of experience in navigation).

Global Positioning System — GPS

The Global Positioning System receives simultaneous signals from several satellites orbiting the earth and uses them to compute the current position of the GPS receiver. The system works anywhere on the planet. GPS is the greatest breakthrough in navigation since the invention of the compass. It works in poor visibility, when other methods fail. Some common functions of GPS receivers include:

> Determination of location
> Direction and distance of the current position in relation to a previously set reference point along the route
> Your course and travel speed
> Optical guidance to the next way point

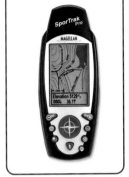

Global Positioning System — GPS

While GPS cannot replace maps, a compass and an altimeter, it is a valuable tool to complement traditional methods of navigation. A GPS receiver cannot make up for a lack of practical and theoretical navigation skills. For expeditions and longer tours, it is advisable to use GPS receivers (a spare unit is a good idea, as well as spare batteries). GPS data is ideal for directing a search-and-rescue (SAR) team to the exact location of an accident. Currently GPS accuracy is approximately to 66 feet (20 meters) horizontally and 164 feet (50 meters) vertically. Simple GPS receivers are available at prices starting from $100.

Cell Phones

Cell phones can be very useful in the backcountry, and most outdoor folks now consider them a part of their standard equipment. As long as you are able to receive a signal from a **cell phone tower**, it is easy to call for help in case of emergency.

Unfortunately cell phone service is very limited in most backcountry areas of North America (unlike in Europe), but near ski areas you should be able to use your cell phone most of the time to get assistance in case of an accident.

If you receive only a weak signal, it often helps to proceed to an elevated spot, where reception may be strong enough to permit an emergency call. That way you may be able to get help faster than by hiking to the closest ski lift.

Whether or not it makes sense to bring your cell phone on a tour depends on your destination. Depending on the area where you will be traveling, reception may be good, sufficient or virtually nonexistent. To make a free emergency call, dial 911 if you are anywhere in the United States and 112 if you are in Europe. In Canada, you may have to call the nearest police station, since there are areas that are not covered by 911 (for more emergency numbers, see Chapter 9).

: Additional Equipment

In recent years some very smart folks from the outdoor industry have developed a number of useful items to enhance freeriding safety. You may consider using these items together with your standard safety equipment.

ABS — Avalanche Airbag System

This ABS system is integrated in a freeride backpack and has been on the market for several years. Airbag packs are available in sizes ranging from 600 to 3,000 cubic inches (10 to 50 liters).

If you notice that a slide has been triggered, you pull a release handle that, within two seconds, inflates two airbags to a volume of 4,500 cubic inches (75 liters) each. These airbags can pull you up to the surface of the slide, keep you afloat and stop you from being buried under the snow, in most cases. Extensive tests and experiences with real-life situations have yielded very positive results. Since the airbag system can keep you on the snow surface or at least avoid complete burial, it significantly increases your chances of surviving an avalanche accident. Of course an avalanche airbag can never guarantee survival — an avalanche release is always a life-threatening situation! An airbag system is no excuse for taking a higher risk.

Remember that the airbag must be triggered by the rider — a fast reaction is a precondition for effective use. At a price of approximately $600, an avalanche airbag system may not be a bargain, but it is the only system for actively avoiding a burial in a slide.

ABS — avalanche airbag system

Avalung

The Avalung allows a buried person to breathe under the snow without additional oxygen, simply by filtering air out of the snow. Even compacted avalanche snow contains a minimum of 50 percent air.

The Avalung allows you to breathe oxygen-rich air through a mouthpiece that is connected to a filter system at the front of the Avalung vest and expel low-oxygen air through a valve on your back. For the system to work, it is crucial that you put the mouthpiece into your mouth fast enough and manage to keep it there while you are buried. The Avalung can complement your standard safety equipment; it cannot replace it! It can only help expand the timeframe for successful rescue.

Avalung (by Black Diamond)

Avalanche Ball

This system consists of a collapsible ball that is stowed in a pocket attached to a back-pack. The ball is connected by a 20-foot (six-meter) cord to a belt around the rider's waist. Similar to the airbag system, the ball must be manually deployed by pulling a rip cord. The ball then folds out and jumps out of its pocket. Due to its low weight, it remains on the snow surface and helps locate the victim at the other end of the cord. If the ball is released in time, it is theoretically no longer necessary to use a transceiver for tracking the victim. Nevertheless we believe that it cannot replace a transceiver and must not be used instead of one.

Recco System

The Recco system consists of a little reflector that is sewn into the rider's clothing (or attached to a ski boot). The reflector returns a signal from a Recco detector and helps locate the buried person. Many ski areas are now equipped with Recco detectors. However, this is a purely passive system and offers no opportunity for companion rescue. Recco detectors

Recco reflector

are only at the disposal of organized rescue teams. By the time an organized team reaches the location of the accident, you may already be dead. Therefore, the Recco system may be used in addition to a transceiver but never instead of it. But since the little reflectors can help save your life, they are better than nothing.

>>Chapter 5

: What to Do in Case of an Accident—

Rescue and First Aid

"Males, especially young males, always have, and most likely always will have, the inexorable need to go out into the world and slay dragons. When we go out to slay the avalanche dragon, there will always be a certain percentage who do not come back alive. Testosterone makes the voice deep, the chest hairy, the muscles strong, the ego huge! But the avalanche doesn't care about these things. Avalanches hew down the strong and weak alike, but avalanches do not hew down the aware and the unaware alike."

Bruce Tremper, Avalanche Expert

Rider and photographer in a massive slab avalanche. Ralf Hochhauser △ Dachstein, Austria Stefan Ehrenhuber

: What to Do if Caught in an Avalanche

Despite all safety measures, you can never completely exclude the possibility of an avalanche accident. If you get caught in a slide, you can still adopt a series of measures that can increase your chances of survival. But it is always difficult to plan how to react in an extreme situation. Therefore you should...

> > **Try everything you can to avoid being buried in an avalanche!**

Don't just think, "It'll be alright." Accept that there is always the possibility of triggering a slide. Your life may depend on your fast reaction.

> If you feel uneasy, turn back or avoid the suspect situation. If that is impossible, wrap a scarf, neck gaiter or other cloth around your nose and mouth. Most avalanche victims are suffocated.

> If you find yourself in the path of an oncoming avalanche, yell to draw attention to yourself.

> If possible, try to ride out of the slide. If you reach the edge of the moving snow masses, you have a better chance to remain on the surface or at least get only partially buried.

> If it is too late to ride out of the danger zone, try to kick off your skis or snowboard, as these act like anchors and pull you even deeper under the snow. Snowboarders have a disadvantage over skiers, because there is no self-releasing system available for most snowboard bindings.

> Try to grab onto trees, rocks or other obstacles to slow yourself down as the avalanche carries you down the slope.

> When the enormous forces in an avalanche kick you around and push you down, try everything you can to remain afloat. It is particularly important that you try to keep your head above the surface. When the slide slows down, make a very strong effort to get to the surface. If that doesn't work, put your arms in front of your face like a boxer and try to create an air pocket.

> Try everything you can to make a breathing space! If you should be among the few victims who manage to do so, you have a good chance of getting enough oxygen to survive until you're rescued.

> When the snow comes to a standstill, relax and try to remain calm. Don't shout, as most probably no one will hear you and you will only waste valuable oxygen. Find out which way is up by spitting or urinating. That way a rescue dog can also smell you better and you can be located faster if you are not carrying a transceiver.

> If you are close to the surface, try to free yourself. Try to attract attention by shouting, but only if you hear a rescuer immediately above you. Though you may hear people talking on the snow surface very clearly, your chances of being heard from underneath the snow are very slim.

Though help arrives too late for many victims, you should never give up hope. There is always the chance of a miracle. Many victims who were believed dead were ultimately rescued against all odds. One person was even saved after 13 days in an avalanche.

Chances of Surviving an Avalanche Accident

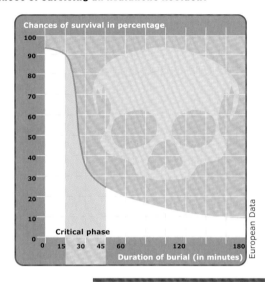

Companion rescue is the key. It takes an average of two to three hours to several days (unless you are next to a ski hill) for an organized rescue team to arrive on location. For most victims, this is too late.

The chances of survival decrease drastically as time progresses. Time is life!

Companion Rescue

The bottom line is that only immediate rescue by other group members provides a reasonable chance of survival. Your companions are the only ones who can immediately start searching without losing precious time. Every freerider is therefore not only responsible for himself or herself, but also for his or her companions. In case of an emergency, this responsibility cannot be transferred to somebody else!

A precondition for fast and effective help is that everybody in the group be equipped with a transceiver. The chances of survival diminish so quickly as time progresses that every minute counts. If the victim is located and uncovered within 15 minutes of burial, the chances of survival are high.

Companion rescue can be successful only if everybody in the group is equipped with a transceiver, a shovel and a probe. Learn and regularly practice how to use the transceiver. There is nothing worse than being the only one who could help and not knowing what to do. So, **practice, practice, practice!**

Since each avalanche accident is different, there is no single standard procedure. However, these general guidelines can help you make the right decisions in a life-threatening situation. If someone is buried in an avalanche, the first thing to do is get an overview of the situation. It is vital to determine how many individuals were buried. Remain calm, don't panic! Make your decisions carefully, don't run off and start searching in a disorganized way.

Observe the following procedure in all avalanche accidents:

> 1. **Make sure you and the rest of the group are safe**
> 2. **Count heads**
> 3. **Establish last-seen points**
> 4. **Determine a safe spot, in case of further avalanches**
> 5. **Organize your group efficiently**
> 6. **Search with beacons, eyes and ears**
> 7. **Search the entire avalanche deposition zone**

If several people are available, the most experienced should take charge and give clear instructions for rescue procedures. If only one person remains, he or she has the burden of carrying out all necessary tasks alone.

The next step is to switch all transceivers to receive. Otherwise, you will get strong signals, but not from the buried person. Then establish search teams based on the number of buried persons. The most experienced group members should begin with a beacon search, while the rest of the group should get their probes, shovels, and first-aid kits ready and then follow the searchers out onto the avalanche debris. If a large rescue team is available, one or, better, two persons can be sent to summon an organized rescue team (see "Calling for Help," on page 119). If you carry a cell phone or two-way radio, you can call for help. If the group is small, all members should participate in the search, since companion rescue provides by far the best chances of survival.

If there is sufficient manpower, the leader should remain in a central spot and coordinate the search. He can scan the snow surface from his vantage point for the victims and their equipment, determine search corridors and keep an eye on the avalanche path for possible hazard from further slides. The leader may ask a helper to store material in a suitable safe place to avoid possible accidents in case of a helicopter rescue (see page 120) and to call for help.

Once a victim is located, try to uncover the head first, immediately clear the airway and check breathing.

The leader must make sure that only one beacon searcher looks for each missing person. Several searchers close together confuse each other. There is a strong tendency to bunch up once several searchers have received a signal — stay organized. Assign people with probes and shovels to each signal that is being received.

Once you have uncovered someone who was buried, switch off the victim's beacon in order to avoid interference with other signals. If you believe that no other person was buried, check the whole deposition zone with the transceiver. If you cannot receive another signal, turn all beacons back on transmitting (in case of subsequent avalanches). Then check the state of the victim by following first-aid procedures (see "First-Aid Procedures After an Avalanche Accident," on page 119).

Companion rescue must be organized efficiently and methodically from the beginning to leave a possibility for a later search by organized rescue teams with dogs. Since rescue dogs use their sense of smell to locate victims, it is vital to avoid contaminating the snow surface with food scraps, urine, spit, cigarette butts and other liquids or substances that could confuse the dogs. Employing search dogs in a contaminated deposition zone is useless! Statistically there is a 2:3 chance of successful companion rescue, while the chances of being rescued by a dog are at a mere 1:6 (European data).

Locating a Victim

> Eye-and-Ear Search

The beacon searchers who are first out on the deposition zone should also make a visual and auditory search of the entire avalanche area. Chances are that the victim remained on the surface or was only partially buried. Even partially submerged victims often don't manage to free themselves, as the snow becomes hard as cement as soon as the slide stops. Depending on their position, even partially buried victims may suffocate. Watch out for pieces of equipment on the surface of the deposition area and pull them out of the snow to check whether the victim is still attached to them. If you don't find the person, put these objects back in the place where you found them. They can provide valuable clues for rescue teams.

If you are unable to spot a partially buried person, you may still hear noises. Keep your ears open for shouts or moaning. If the lost person is not found immediately, it is crucial to mark the last-seen point.

People tend to be buried in places where there is a bigger deposition of snow: on benches, in front of trees or obstacles, or very close to the toe of the deposit. If the victim was not wearing a transceiver, start looking and probing in those likely areas downhill from the last-seen point, keeping the flow lines of the avalanche in mind.

> Beacon Search

The fastest and easiest way to find a buried person who carries a transceiver is the induction method. A **coarse search** (primary phase) starts by switching all transceivers to receive (put analog beacons on the highest volume setting). Now walk uphill from the bottom of the deposition zone toward the avalanche's starting zone, at a distance of 60 feet (20 meters) between searchers. Search along the entire width of the deposition zone; don't move closer than 30 feet (10 meters) to its edges. If you are the only searcher, zigzag up the avalanche path. Make sure your strip lines are spaced closer than 60 feet (20 meters) to receive a signal even in case of a very deep burial or an unfavorable antenna position. It is usually no problem to pick up a signal.

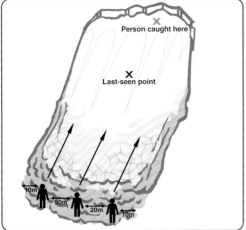

Searchers move uphill toward the avalanche's starting zone, at a distance of 60 feet (20 meters) between them. Don't exceed this maximum spacing, to make sure that you can receive a signal, even if the antenna is in a position that reduces the beacon's range. Maximum distance to the edges of the deposition zone is 30 feet (10 meters).

A single searcher zigzags uphill. Again, maximum distance is 60 feet (20 meters) between switchbacks and 30 feet (10 meters) to the edges of the deposition zone.

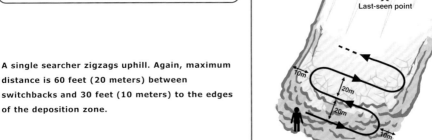

When you pick up a signal, you can proceed with a **fine search** (secondary phase). If you are using **analog transceivers**, only one trained person should continue searching for each signal. All other beacons should be turned to minimum volume. **Make sure that no beacon is set on transmitting!** The remaining rescuers should get ready for probing, digging and first-aid procedures. Multiple burials naturally require several searchers.

Hold your analog transceiver horizontally at waist level and always reorient it by turning your whole body, not just the beacon.

Establish the direction of the strongest signal and start walking. When the signal has reached the maximum (analog beacons), turn down the volume. Proceed in the direction of the strongest signal until you reach the maximum again and repeat the process until you have reached the lowest volume setting for pinpointing the victim. Once you have reached the maximum at this lowest setting, continue a few steps until the signal gets weaker. Then return to the spot of the strongest signal and start pinpointing.

The fine search with a **digital transceiver** is facilitated by a visual display that directs the searcher to the victim. These models do not require changing the volume setting. Arrows or LEDs on the display indicate the direction and approximate distance to the buried person. The closer you get to the victim, the more accurate and important the distance on the display becomes. Some models start beeping when you get really close to the victim. Once the display of the digital transceiver indicates that you are directly above the buried person, you may start pinpointing.

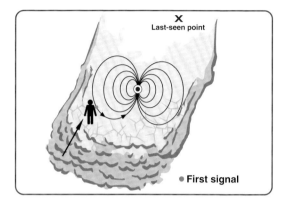

The fine search (secondary search phase) begins when the first signal is picked up. Only the most experienced person continues the beacon search by following the induction line to the point of the strongest signal. The remaining group members get ready for probing, digging and first-aid procedures.

When **pinpointing**, move your beacon in straight lines over the snow surface. Bend down so the beacon is really low, and shuffle your feet along so you don't lift the beacon off the surface. Mark the spot of the strongest signal. Move the transceiver at a right angle over this spot in both directions (like a cross). The person is buried under the spot from which the signal fades in all directions on an analog beacon or the lowest distance displayed on a digital beacon.

If a person is buried very deep, the maximum signal on an analog transceiver fades slowly as you move away from the loudest spot, whereas a rapidly fading signal indicates shallow burial. Digital transceivers display a fairly accurate estimate of the depth of burial. If you find two or even four points with a maximum signal, the person is located right in between these points.

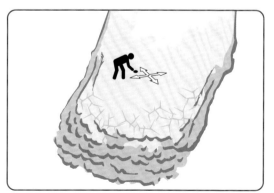

Make sure that you have found the strongest signal by moving the analog transceiver crosswise until the signal fades again. Save time by using a probe for determining the exact position of the victim. Leave the probe in place after making contact.

In order to save vital time, always confirm the victim's exact position with a probe.

Practical Examples of Fine Search and Pinpointing

The signal of your digital transceiver indicates that your buried companion is only 10 meters (30 feet) away. As you move along the induction line and get ever closer, the numbers grow smaller: 10, 9, 8 meters, the beacon now displays the distance at half-meter steps, 2.5, 2, 1.5, 1. After you take one more step, the distance on the display rises to 1.5 meters: You are obviously moving away from your companion. You continue for another step or two to make sure that the signal keeps getting weaker and then return to the point of the strongest signal (the lowest distance on the display). Now you move your transceiver away from that spot at right angles to both sides until you have found the closest distance. Use your probe to confirm that your companion is buried there. If you start digging only half a meter away, you can lose 15 to 20 minutes!

Probing

Push the probe into the snowpack in front of you. Be attentive to any resistance, but push hard enough to penetrate to deeper levels. Wear gloves, as the warmth of your bare hands may cause icy lumps to form around the probe and your sweat may confuse search dogs. Keep pushing the probe into the snow until you feel a soft, spongy resistance. Once you have made contact, leave the probe in place and start digging. Don't worry — you will know when you hit a person.

A rescue team practices probing.
☞ **Raimund Mayr**

Final Phase of Rescue

After probe contact, you'll know the exact position and depth of burial (most probes have one-foot or 40-cm markings along their length, to determine depth of burial).
The deeper the person is buried, the wider you have to dig the hole, or you will be unable to continue digging at a certain depth. The hole also needs to be large enough to excavate the victim. Try to dig down to the person from the side, particularly on slopes, and first uncover the head. Don't dig right down from the top, as you may destroy the victim's air pocket.

First-Aid Procedures After an Avalanche Accident

Always uncover the head first. While others are still digging, check the victim's airways. If there is any snow, blood, or vomit in there, clean it out. It is impossible to do CPR on a victim that is at the bottom of a deep hole, so make the hole big enough! Never assume a victim is dead if you can't see them breathing. Their breathing may be extremely shallow and hard to see. Be very careful of spinal injuries, and use great caution when moving an avalanche victim.

Act calmly and with consideration. Particular care is required if…

> The person was buried for a long period of time.
> The snow is wet.
> The patient was already exhausted before burial.

In these cases the patient's body temperature may have dropped considerably. A safety system within the human body gives priority to vital organs for blood supply and reduces blood flow to the periphery to ensure that the brain and vital organs can keep functioning. This leads to a drop in temperature in the periphery of the victim's body. If a patient in this condition is moved too much, this cold blood may reach the core and trigger irregular heart rhythms and circulatory collapse. See the sections on hypothermia (at page 125).

Organized Rescue

Calling for Help

If a visual and auditory search followed by a careful and thorough transceiver search were unsuccessful and no signal was detected — perhaps the buried person was not wearing a beacon — you should immediately call for professional help. If a sufficient number of people are available, call for assistance immediately after the accident. A prerequisite for sending anyone for help is knowing if an organized rescue team can be on location within a reasonable amount of time. If, for instance, you know that it is a day's walk to the closest place from where you can call for assistance, there is no other choice but to remain on site and try everything you can to help the victims.

Never give up companion rescue unless you are absolutely sure that you are unable to locate the victims without help from outside. If you carry a cell phone and if you can get service, call for help as soon as possible. You can call 911 from anywhere in the United States. In Canada, 911 may or may not work. In many of Canada's remote areas, you have to call the police first. Unfortunately, cell phones often don't work in the backcountry. Therefore, you may be forced to depend on your own resources for locating the victims.

It is up to you to decide when to give up and call for professional rescue. Depending on the distance to the closest spot from where you can call for assistance, organized rescue may be the very last resort or even no option at all.

SOS Signal

The SOS signal uses the Morse code for the letters SOS: - - - – – – - - -, that is, three short (acoustic or optical) signals, followed by three long and another three short signals. If no suitable signaling device such as a mirror or whistle is available, use any artificial modi-fication of the environment that attracts attention.

Helicopter Rescue

Before the helicopter can land, you have to stow all gear in a suitable depot. Collect and secure all your gear in a hole approximately five feet (1.5 meters) long by three feet (1 meter) wide and two feet (0.5 meter) deep, depending on the amount that needs to be stowed. If you cannot find a suitable hollow, you will have to dig a hole in a convenient spot. Make sure that all objects that could be drawn into the helicopter's rotor during landing or take off are safely stored in the hole. Backpacks, jackets and other loose objects must be placed at the bottom and covered with skis and snowboards. While the helicopter is approaching you can lay down on top of the boards to secure the cache. If your gear is not secured properly, the downwash from the rotor may send snowboards flying around like spears and cause injury or damage to the helicopter.

It is important to locate the cache at a safe distance from the landing site. The landing zone must be free of obstacles over an area of 20 square yards (20 square meters) and should be about 30 feet (10 meters) from the site of the accident. Warning: Any overhead cables must be indicated to the pilot!

Keep visual contact with the pilot during landing. Never go around the back of the helicopter and always wait for the rotors to come to a standstill before you approach the craft. The area within 25 yards or meters of the helicopter is dangerous!

Signaling to the pilot.
YES. Landing possible / "We need help."
NO. Landing not possible / "We don't need help."

Warning: The pilot has a limited field of view and may need directions for landing. Stay where you can be seen until the helicopter has safely landed.

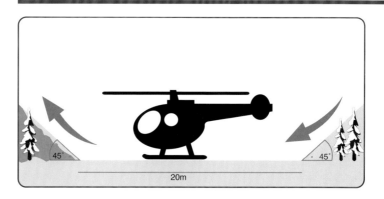

Organized Rescue

Though organized rescue is carried out by experienced professionals, it is no alternative to companion rescue. By the time the rescue team arrives at the site of the accident, it is usually too late to recover anyone alive. In Europe it takes an average of 30 to 45 minutes, while in North America, unless you are right next to a ski hill, it takes at least two to three hours. It may also take several days. Poor visibility or high winds may hamper helicopter rescue. In such a case, it may be many hours before a rescue team arrives.

If the buried person is not carrying a transceiver or Recco (see Chapter 4), a search dog is the best chance for rescue. For the dog to be effective, the deposition surface must be uncontaminated (free from food scraps, urine and other liquids, and cigarette butts). If the dog is unsuccessful, probing the entire avalanche area is the next option. If probing doesn't locate the victim, which is often the case with very large avalanches or a very deep burial, the searchers dig ditches across the entire deposition zone.

In order to avoid the enormous costs of a false alarm, anybody who observes an avalanche or triggers a slide should always inform ski area personnel or relevant authorities. If you have triggered an avalanche and nobody was injured, it is better to inform the ski patrol and face their anger than risk causing a search-and-rescue team to set off for nothing.

A catastrophic avalanche

⌖Bavarian Avalanche Warning Service

⁞ First Aid

Unfortunately, most freeriders don't think of first aid until they get involved in an accident, and then it is usually too late. Anybody who travels in remote mountain areas should at least have some basic knowledge of first-aid procedures. In an emergency your companions depend on you for competent help, and you on them. Just like the case of companion rescue, our friends' capabilities are our backup and our life insurance.

First-Aid Basics for Freeriders

No theoretical information is ever as good as practical experience. Reading about first aid in a book is like watching a freeride contest on television. You probably found your last first-aid course boring and had the feeling that it didn't teach you anything useful for freeriding. But it is irresponsible to go freeriding without any first-aid skills. The following pages provide some useful tips and information, but this information cannot replace first-aid training. The best thing to do would be to attend advanced wilderness first-aid training or get trained as a wilderness first responder.

What is important?

In freeriding you will mainly be confronted with the following two situations:

> 1. Life-threatening HYPO emergencies
> 2. Minor RICE injuries

It is important that you are able to take the appropriate, life-saving measures in life-threatening situations and treat minor injuries properly to prevent the development of a **HYPO** emergency. The three life-threatening **HYPO** emergencies are:

> Hypovolemia — a decrease in the volume of circulating blood, leading to shock
> Hypoxia — breathing problems, resulting in an oxygen deficiency
> Hypothermia — a subnormal body temperature

Minor injuries include contusions, sprains and other so-called sports injuries that require the **RICE** treatment.

> Rest or immobilization
> Ice
> Compression
> Elevation

Let's have a closer look at these two categories of first-aid situations.

1. Life Threatening Conditions

Most fatal outdoor accidents involve shock, breathing problems or hypothermia. If you manage to avoid these conditions or recognize them and give the right treatment, you may be able to save a person's life.

Hypovolemia — Leading to Shock

Shock is a life-threatening malfunction of the circulatory system. When you are in a state of shock, the circulating blood volume is insufficient to deliver enough oxygen to the 10 trillion cells of your body. Relevant causes for freeriders include:

> Severe bleeding (e.g., in connection with fractures after serious falls)
> Severe dehydration
> Allergic reactions (anaphylactic shock)

(The type of psychological reaction we colloquially call a shock will not be discussed here, as it does not represent a life-threatening condition.)

To recognize hypovolemia and shock, watch out for these symptoms:

> **Cold, pale, clammy skin** (allergic or anaphylactic shock: red skin all over the body).
> **Weak, rapid pulse** (severe shock: pulse is not or hardly palpable at the wrist).
> **Cold sweat, shivering**
> **Slow reaction to compression of the fingertip or earlobe.** Squeeze the patient's earlobe or finger at the nail until it turns white and observe how long it takes for the skin to turn pink again. If it takes longer than two seconds, circulation is seriously impaired. This may be caused by hypovolemia.
> **Restlessness, anxiety, trembling.**

> These symptoms also accompany the relatively harmless psychogenic shock. The decisive difference is the presence of an injury (e.g., severe bleeding).

What to do?

The general recommendation of elevating the victim's legs (shock treatment position) is not always appropriate and can be harmful if the patient suffered fractures of the legs, pelvis or chest and in cases of difficult breathing or head injury.

Treatment for shock should always include a variety of measures:

> Eliminate or mitigate all causes as quickly as possible (stop the bleeding, prevent dehydration).
> In the absence of the above-mentioned injuries, elevate the patient's legs.
> Keep the patient warm (see "Hypothermia") but don't apply external heat.
> Provide psychological assistance, comfort and reassurance to the patient.
> Constantly monitor the patient's pulse and do the fingernail or earlobe test.
> Call for professional help (two-way radio or cell phone) and prepare evacuation.

Scenario

Your companion fell off a cliff and badly hurt his leg on a rock. You examine him and it is obvious that professional help is needed. His leg may be broken. Your cell phone is not working, and it will take half an hour minimum to get back to the closest ski lift. The care and comfort you provide for your friend already made him feel better, and he is confident that he could stick it out for an hour until help arrives, even though his leg hurts badly. You put his leg in the most comfortable position and wrap a foil blanket around him. Any tea left in the thermos flask is reserved for the patient. You are getting ready to get help when you become aware that the leg is swelling rapidly. You notice that your friend is getting pale and he says that the pain feels different. His pulse is at 120 beats per minute, even though he seems relatively calm.

These symptoms should ring the alarm bells! Your friend is suffering from hypovolemia caused by internal bleeding in his injured leg and may easily lose four pints (two liters) of blood. The situation is serious; time is precious! A snowcat will not do, the patient must be evacuated by helicopter as soon as possible. Go for help quickly (but safely!) and continually check whether you can get through on your cell phone. Organize a helicopter rescue as fast as possible.

Hypoxia or Breathing Problems

We cannot live without oxygen. It takes only two minutes for the first brain cells to die when they are not properly supplied with oxygen. There are many possible causes for breathing problems. Here are a few:

> **Obstruction of the airway by the tongue or by vomit in the case of an unconscious patient (e.g., as a consequence of a head injury)**
> **Obstruction of the airway after burial in an avalanche**
> **Impaired chest movement after burial in a wet-snow avalanche**
> **Chest injuries (e.g., broken ribs)**
> **Acute illnesses, such as asthma**

First aid is absolutely vital in the case of breathing problems, as professional medical assistance almost always arrives too late. Fortunately the necessary measures are fairly simple.

Case 1: The patient responds and has breathing difficulties

Bring the patient to an upright position and reach around the chest from behind. Give instructions for breathing ("breathe in ... breathe out ... breathe in ...") and apply gentle pressure on the chest during exhalation to calm down the patient and normalize breathing. A calm patient uses less oxygen and can handle the breathing problem better.

Remove or treat the cause. For instance, help asthmatics to take their prescribed asthma spray.

Case 2: The patient is unconscious; breathing is sufficient

In order to keep the airway unobstructed, the patient is put in the recovery position.

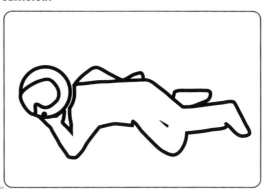

Case 3: The patient is not breathing

If the patient is not breathing, you have to perform CPR. Close the patient's mouth and breathe into his nose. Keep a normal rhythm and depth of breath. Don't "inflate" the patient. If the person has no palpable pulse, you will also have to compress the chest. Proper CPR can be learned only in a first-aid course.

Hypothermia

Hypothermia generally plays a minor role in "regular" first aid. In outdoor activities such as freeriding, it is a major health hazard. While you are working hard on your first-aid tasks, immobilizing broken limbs and preparing evacuation, the patient is lying still and avoiding the smallest movement to ease the pain. The patient's muscles are not producing any heat, and his body temperature drops quickly. Hypothermia is a life-threatening drop in body temperature.

The cause for hypothermia is a loss of energy that the body cannot restore because the person is injured, exhausted or in poor physical condition.

An important factor in connection with hypothermia is **wind chill**. Wind removes heat from the surface of our skin. This heat loss increases dramatically with rising wind speed.

>> Wind Chill

Wind speed	Actual air temperature		
Calm conditions	35° F/2° C	10 °F/-12°C	-10°F/-23°C

Wind speed	Heat loss equal to an air temperature of		
10 mph/16 kmh	22°F/-6°C	-9°F/-23°C	-34°F/ -37°C
20 mph/32 kmh	12°F/-11°C	-24°F/-31°C	-53°F/-47°C
30 mph/48 kmh	6°F/-15°C	-33°F/-36°C	-64°F/-53°C
40 mph/64 kmh	3°F/-16°C	-37°F/-38°C	-69°F/-56°C

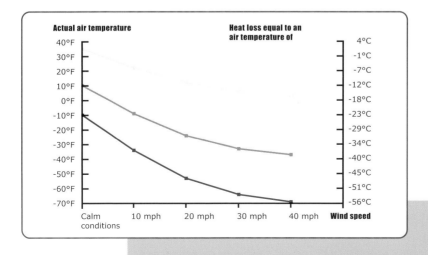

Recognizing Hypothermia

Treatment of mild hypothermia is significantly different from treatment of severe cases. However, both are intimately related.

Mild hypothermia — increased physiological activity

> Shivering
> Cold, pale skin (sometimes grayish, bluish)
> Rapid pulse
> Pain or numbness of limbs

Severe hypothermia — reduced physiological activity

> Shivering stopped, muscular rigidity
> Patient becomes increasingly apathetic and sleepy
> Weak pulse
> Decreased sensation of pain
> Slow and shallow breathing, sometimes irregular

Severe hypothermia can cause death.

If blood with a temperature below 80 degrees Fahrenheit (27 degrees Celsius) reaches the heart, the circulatory system collapses.

Treatment of Mild Hypothermia

If the patient is still responsive, able to move and hold a cup of tea, he or she is suffering from mild hypothermia. The body is still trying to produce heat by shivering and rapid pulse. Common sense tells you what to do:

> Remove wet clothes (in a place sheltered from the wind) and replace with dry clothes. Warning: Patients who complain of feeling too stiff to take their clothes off may already suffer from severe hypothermia. In this case it is extremely dangerous to move the patient at all.
> Wrap a jacket or, if possible, a sleeping bag around the patient and over that, a foil blanket or bivy bag. Provide shelter from the wind, and cover the patient's head with a wooly hat or hood.
> Supply the body with energy. Warm, sweet liquids are particularly suitable, as carbohydrates can easily be converted into energy. Chemical heat packs are not truly effective but provide reasonable relief if placed under the armpits or in the groin.
> Create a human hot water bottle. Have one or two persons lie with the patient in a bivy bag or foil blanket.
> Important: Never give the patient alcohol! Alcohol causes further heat loss.

Treatment of Severe Hypothermia

The main objective of treatment is to avoid a sudden drop in body temperature when the patient is moved during rescue procedures. This sudden drop can lead to severe complications that may even be fatal. This is what happens in such a case:

The extremities of a severely hypothermic patient have a considerably lower temperature than the patient's core. If the patient is moved or if excessive external heat is applied, blood circulation to the periphery is increased and the cold blood returning to the core causes the core temperature to drop by several degrees and even fall below the critical level of 80 degrees Fahrenheit (27 degrees Celsius).

The following measures must be taken to avoid this effect:

> **Do not move the patient!**
> **Do not take off wet clothes.** It may be possible to remove clothes carefully by cutting them off.
> **Do not transport the patient**, except in case of immediate danger (avalanches, falling rocks or ice).
> If the patient must be sheltered in a snow hole due to very adverse weather conditions or if it takes a long time for rescue teams to arrive, make sure that **the patient remains in a horizontal position.**
> **Do not elevate the patient's legs! No shock treatment position!**
> Do not give the patient anything to eat or drink. The severely hypothermic patient is semiconscious or unconscious and could choke. A patient who cannot hold a cup of tea is not sufficiently alert to drink.
> **In case of respiratory or circulatory arrest, it is absolutely vital to perform resuscitation!** CPR procedures must be kept up until the patient arrives at the hospital.

Scenario:

It's an extremely cold day after a massive dump. The snow is just perfect, and you and your friends are caught in the "white rush." You're pretty much exhausted already, but conditions are simply incredible. Far out-of-bounds, you suddenly find yourselves at a drop-off and have to turn back. Nobody has snowshoes, and trail-breaking uphill in all that powder is extremely strenuous. One of your buddies is struggling. He is not in the best physical condition, and after three hours of hard hiking, he is finished. He sits down in the snow, totally exhausted and refuses to move any farther. In such a situation, it is important to think carefully and make the right decisions. The best thing to do is to let the strongest person in the group continue alone to get help. Bundle the patient up in dry insulation, and let him slip into a bivy bag with a warm person. That way he can easily survive for a few hours until help arrives. Try to cheer your buddy up, keep him reassured and give him some hot tea and chocolate. The person who sets out to get help should make sure not to lose orientation and be able to guide rescuers to the victim.

>> Sports Injuries — RICE

Let's have a look at those strains, sprains and other minor injuries that don't threaten a person's life but can ground you during the season. This is not about anatomy; all you need to remember is the RICE treatment, which is suitable for all of these minor injuries. Almost every strain, sprain or contusion involves tissue damage. The tissue reacts by depositing fluids in the intercellular space, which causes swelling. Damage of small blood vessels leads to bruises. Swelling and bruises are painful. This pain makes sense from a biological point of view, as it forces you to rest the injured limb. Since you want to get back on the slopes as soon as possible, it is a good idea to limit swelling and bruises. The **RICE** treatment can be used for this objective:

Rest
Rest the injured part of the body. A splint may be helpful for that purpose. A SAM splint is very useful for immobilizing an injured foot or hand (see also the "First-Aid Kit and Emergency Equipment" section in Chapter 4).

Ice
Cold packs reduce blood circulation in the injured tissues and alleviate pain. Use crushed ice, snow or chemical cold packs. Do not apply cold packs directly to the skin; place a protective layer (sock, bandana, etc.) below them.

Compression
Apply an elastic wrap to reduce swelling and bruises. Make sure not to cut off healthy blood circulation. Numbness or tingling sensations are a sign that the compression is too tight. Immobilize joints in the position of function (e.g., a foot perpendicular to the leg). Loosen compressions at intervals of 15 to 20 minutes for a few minutes.

Cold pack

protective layer

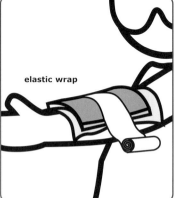

elastic wrap

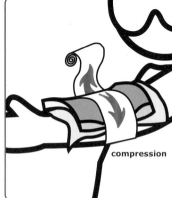

compression

Elevation

Elevating the injured limbs can additionally provide some relief. Elevation feels comfortable for most patients and reduces the formation of bruises.

Don't apply sports creams on fresh injuries!

Sports rubs, such as Voltaren Emulgel, Finalgon, Alleviate Sports Rub, Deep Heat, (heparin, methyl salicylate or nicotinamide creams) are intended to reduce swelling and bruises (the massaging effect of applying the cream is beneficial in itself, as it increases local blood flow). These creams should not be applied during the first few hours after the injury occurred, as they (particularly the massaging action of rubbing the cream on) would aggravate bruising and swelling.

Scenario:

You fall on an icy slope and injure your wrist. You can still move your hand, but it hurts a little. Improvise a cold pack with some snow and wrap your wrist tightly, if possible right on the spot. Descend carefully, and when you are back at home or your hotel, repeatedly apply cold packs and compressions during the ensuing hours. If your wrist doesn't feel better by the next day, go see the doctor. Even if he does not detect any major injuries, your immediate treatment has already helped reduce the recovery time.

As you can see, it is very important to have some basic first-aid knowledge. The best way to prepare yourself for possible emergencies is to take a good practical course in wilderness first aid. After all, you are responsible for your own health and that of your buddies.

Regular CPR training is not sufficient. Get information on courses in your area. Are there any special first-aid courses for freeriding or other outdoor sports? If there aren't any, try to get a few buddies interested, and ask a first-aid organization whether they could run a special course for you. There may be trainers who share your interest in freeriding and are willing to hold a course on the slopes.

⌨Bavarian Avalanche Warning Service △ Chiemgau Alps, Germany

A huge slab avalanche. Two skiers skied down this steep east-facing slope and were killed. The avalanche bulletin had declared High Danger and explicitly warned against east aspects. The accident happened at an elevation of 5,000 feet (1,600 meters).

>> Chapter 6:
: Smart Freeriding and Applied Avalanche Safety

"Lured by the beauty and majesty of the mountains, we set off to play with the white
queen and to celebrate our lives, not to gamble on them. Keep cool and watch out."

Lars Gittermann, Freerider

Thorsten Indra △ Lebanon Lars Gittermann

There is much more to freeriding than surfing down powder slopes. That is just the last act
of the game. Freeriding or skiing is not only riding powder — often you won't find any of
that precious stuff. Don't let the incredible images of freeride movies fool you. They may
make you believe that conditions are always perfect, but what you see in those videos is
often not nearly as enjoyable for the riders as it may seem. And without self-discipline,
experience and training, you won't get anywhere.

   At the end of the season, even the locals can count those special days when everything
was right — powder, fine weather, an acceptable risk and good personal fitness — on the
fingers of one hand. Actually, you don't see a lot of true freeriding in movies. Many
professional riders don't have a lot of snow-how; they have to leave all the critical decisions
to the mountain guides and safety experts. These riders depend on large support teams
behind the scenes. And hiring a helicopter to take you up a mountain and a guide to bring
you safely down doesn't have much to do with true freeriding, either.

We believe that freeriding involves years of dedication, of learning to understand nature in its extreme manifestations and of getting to know yourself. With all the beauty in freeriding, there are also those hairy situations when, sometimes within seconds, sudden danger forces you to make the right life-saving decision. As you know now, there is always a remaining risk attached to every line you pick. That's why "no risk, no fun; no limit, no life" is the essence of freeriding. Never forget that.

: Learn the Basics

> Work on your riding/skiing skills before you leave the ski trails. The back-country is no playground for beginners.

> Take a course! At the very least, take a class in evaluating avalanche hazard, risk management and rescue. Check out your course provider carefully: Is he a seasoned professional or merely somebody who just took his own first avalanche course? The next course should be on backcountry touring and traveling skills (orientation with a map and compass; route finding).

> Apply your acquired knowledge, and don't expect to know everything after a course.

> New skills must be learned, understood and applied in the field. Some practice can be done in the summer (transceiver search, orientation, predicting weather changes). Why not plan a few tours for the coming season in the summer?

> Get started with out-of-bounds riding/skiing in the vicinity of ski areas and gather experience. But don't forget that even there, you may be exposed to avalanche danger. Practice risk management, judging slope inclination and aspect and riding in different terrain and snow conditions.

> Take your first trips to the backcountry with mountain guides, experienced skiers or boarders or commercial operators that run guided tours. This will offer you the opportunity to learn step-by-step, gather experience and ask questions. Freeriding is not a sport to learn by trial and error (unless you have a special agreement with a guardian angel).

> Once you know the basics, you can go on your first tours. Of course, it's a good idea to start with short and easy trips.

> Apart from mental training and good planning, physical fitness naturally plays an important role. Whether it's cycling, swimming, jogging, specific strength training or a balanced diet, there's a lot you can do to get in shape for freeriding. A good level of fitness may save your life in extreme situations.

That's how you become a freerider. With some patience, discipline and good luck, you'll be spending wonderful days in the mountains, surfing fantastic slopes and enjoying the satisfaction of finding your own way through the backcountry and picking the right lines.

Rules of Thumb (see also "Basic Rules for the Backcountry," in Chapter 1)

Even though avalanches are very complex, some simple and practical rules can help you get safely through the winter season without having to become a snow scientist. Of course, these rules of thumb can't guarantee you'll be spared all avalanche accidents, but they do address some fundamental issues that you should always keep in mind.

> Never ride or ski alone.
> No beacon, no ride. Never go freeriding without a transceiver, probe and shovel, and make sure that all your buddies carry them, too.
> At **Considerable** Danger, avoid steep, rocky terrain and don't jump off cornices.
> Steep, shady slopes are mostly critical. The powder is tempting but be careful, these slopes are particularly prone to avalanching.
> Keep a large distance between each of your buddies when hiking. Traverse suspect slopes one at a time.
> On the downhill, always go one at a time. Never ride as a group.
> Keep in control and avoid falls.
> Don't stop on steep sections; ride through them.
> Don't jump off cornices onto wind-loaded slopes.
> Avoid gullies, stay on ridges.

Apply the principle of **fluid riding**. The most experienced rider usually goes first and rides to a previously identified safe spot. The goal is to ride carefully, anticipate dangers and take wide and gentle turns. If the team consists of riders with a similar level of experience, you may consider **leapfrogging**: Discuss the line with your partners and pick a safe spot where the first rider stops; the second rider follows, catches up with the first and continues to the next island of safety, and so on.

Terrain Evaluation

Proactive terrain evaluation, or reading a slope, is the highest art of freeriding. Information gleaned from a map — such as inclination, aspect, slope shape, ground surface and vegetation — must be transferred to the actual slope. Valuable second-hand information from the avalanche bulletin and weather forecast should also be incorporated in the general assessment.

Only when you are able to identify rideable and dangerous slope sections can you adapt your line to the terrain. This proactive attitude is a precondition for adjusting to ever-changing terrain and snow conditions. Proactive freeriding allows you to get the most from the variety of conditions you may find on a single slope. It enables you to take advantage of opportunities like little cornices or jumps and to recognize dangers like icy sections or wind slabs early enough to avoid them or react properly. If you don't adjust your riding to existing conditions and try to force your style upon the mountain, you will soon be taught a painful lesson. No matter how good a rider or skier you are, the mountain is always stronger! Ascents, hikes and rides up the lift offer good opportunities for general terrain evaluation.

Always keep your eyes open for typical danger spots and danger indicators such as:

> Recent avalanching
> Whumpfing sounds and other alarm signs
> Large amounts of fresh windblown snow
> Steep, rocky slopes. Such slopes can be particularly dangerous because the snowpack on them tends to be especially uneven and unstable, especially where perforated by protruding rocks or trees. Protruding objects do not anchor the snow, but weaken it (like the perforations between sheets of toilet paper), resulting in the frequent release of slab avalanches between rocks or trees.
> Steep slopes with northwest and north to east aspects
> Steep slopes that end at cliffs. Such slopes are particularly dangerous, just because they expose you to the general risk of falling off a cliff. The snowpack is often less stable due to poor compressive support, and even a small slide or sluff may sweep you off your feet and carry you over the drop.
> Slopes below wind-deceleration areas, such as saddles and passes that favor wind loading
> On the downwind sides of ridges and crests, where you'll often find large areas of wind-deposited snow
> Gullies and couloirs, particularly tapered gullies (funnel effect) and depressions
> V-shaped channels (like creek beds at the bottom of slopes), which can become death traps where even a small slide can bury you very deeply
> Steep, open slopes without significant terrain features (like broad ledges) that could stabilize the snow cover. Protruding rocks, however, make a slope less stable!
> Cornices, which always indicate dangerous wind loading
> Ripples and dunes on the snow surface — indicators of windblown snow
> Sastrugi, which signifies strong wind activity

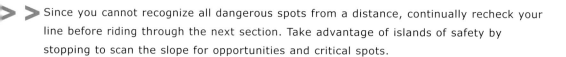

Since you cannot recognize all dangerous spots from a distance, continually recheck your line before riding through the next section. Take advantage of islands of safety by stopping to scan the slope for opportunities and critical spots.

: Safe Meeting Points

Always pick spots that offer maximum safety for regrouping (of course, there is no such thing as a 100 percent safe spot). Good meeting points can be found on ridges, knolls or behind large rocks.

When riding extreme terrain, manage the sluff!   ⊙Red Bull/Greg Epstein △ Alaska

: Riding/Skiing in Difficult Terrain and Snow Conditions

Here are a few tips and tricks for riding in different conditions. Good technique can help you enjoy even difficult snow and terrain and make your riding safer and more fluent. Of course, reading a book can never replace actual freeriding experience or a practical course.

Powder Snow

In order to enjoy the real surfing sensation offered by powder snow, you should first develop a solid skill base on ski trails. To master powder, all you need is a little bit more speed. Once you get the hang of it, you'll see that nothing (with the possible exception of flying) can be better.

Powder turns should be wide and fast and well controlled. Don't go for an aggressive kamikaze style; use a defensive surfing style, without bouncing too much between turns, to minimize stress to the snowpack. Avoid tight rhythmic turns with strong up and down movements, which places a high amount of stress on the snowpack. This is easy for snowboarders to do, but difficult for skiers.

On extremely steep terrain, riders are often chased by sluffs. Sluffs are mostly little loose-snow slides triggered by the riders' turns. In steep terrain, they quickly pick up speed. Once they reach a critical mass, sluffs can knock even experienced riders or skiers off their feet. From time to time, you will have to get out of the way of the sluff and let it overtake you. Simply ride up a crest or spine while the sluff drains through the gully below, or move across the fall line to let the sluff pass you by. Then continue your line.

Steep Terrain and Icy Conditions

Steep terrain starts at an angle of 30 degrees. Slopes steeper than 35 degrees are potentially very dangerous in case of a fall. Although such slopes can be easy to descend when covered with powder, even experienced freeriders and freeskiers may reach the limit of their skills when conditions turn icy. This is particularly true for snowboarders, as they cannot rely on the long, effective edges and superior power transfer of skis. In extremely steep terrain, you can increase the upward motion that starts a turn and do jump turns, so that your board or skis lose contact with the ground while you change edges. Make sure that you always have good edge grip on icy snow. Under these conditions, your edges are your life insurance.

Whether a snowboarder or a skier, you should try to adopt a gentle and controlled riding style. It is important to avoid falls at all costs. On slopes steeper than 35 degrees, it's extremely hard to slow down and regain control after a fall (see also "Falls," on page 143). Proper technique enables you to manage even steep and icy slopes without any big problems. Ski areas are good places to improve your riding skills in difficult terrain. When all the powder is tracked, you have the perfect playground to practice controlled riding in changing conditions. Particularly for snowboarders, these conditions are very challenging and ideal for training fast responses and coordination, as well as for testing the strength of your knees and ankles.

> > Don't be ashamed to play safe — the safest line is the best line.

⏏Richard Walch △ New Zealand ⚡Marco Lutz

Couloirs and Gullies

Steep gullies are particularly unforgiving because any mistake can have fatal consequences. If you fall, you may trigger a slide. In steep terrain, even a sluff with a depth of only a few inches can sweep you over a cliff, particularly when you have your skis or board at a right angle to the fall line, presenting a large surface likely to be dragged downhill by the sliding snow. Falls are very dangerous because you risk hitting a rock. Wearing a helmet and back protector is highly recommended.

Spring Snow and Firn

After powder, spring snow and firn are probably second best. If you like going fast, this is the right stuff. Beware of shady spots (often found around trees or rocks), where the surface may still be icy and send you for a hard landing if you're caught off guard.

Descending in Adverse Conditions

Even thorough planning cannot guarantee that you won't find yourself in adverse conditions from time to time. Possible causes include a sudden change in the weather, poor visibility or fog, steep icy slopes, bad timing, exhaustion or injuries. In these cases, it is all about getting home safely, even if the style factor is close to zero. Go slowly to save strength and reduce the risk.

> > **Important:** Think carefully, don't panic and don't make hasty decisions. In critical situations your best chance for a happy end is to thoroughly consider all options and make a careful decision. Better to hit the bivvy bag than a rock, even if you don't close your eyes all night long!

Riding Through Forests

It is a common and potentially deadly mistake to believe that there are no avalanches in forests. It's true that fewer avalanches release in forests than on open slopes, but once a slab is triggered, it can run almost unhindered through the trees, especially if they are far apart. If you take a ride, the risk of death is much higher in forests. Being wrapped around a tree trunk by the incredible forces in an avalanche is extremely dangerous.

Actually, the snow tends to be more stable in the trees because the snowpack is modified by tree bombs that fall off the branches and because a lot of snow gets held up by the canopy. The anchoring effect of the stems is secondary. Conifers (except larches, which lose their needles in winter) do a better job of stabilizing the snowpack than deciduous trees.

A forest is safe with regard to avalanches only when it is so dense that it is impossible to ride or ski between the trees. Lightly timbered slopes often attract riders in poor visibility and during snowfall. Unfortunately trees are rather immobile and tend to be harder than your head. Nonetheless, you may damage the trees with your board or skis. In the harsh environments around the timberline, even minor damage can eventually kill a tree.

In North America, where the timberline is much higher than it is in Europe, forest rides are sometimes the only way to get some powder. This is even more true for the West Coast, where poor visibility due to heavy snowfall frequently forces riders into forests.

Because of the dangers lurking in the woods, you should generally ride more slowly and carefully. This helps increase your own life span (even small trees are often amazingly hard) as well as those of the trees.

Beware of tree wells, which often form around tree trunks and can be more than 10 feet deep. If you fall head first into one and your skis or board gets caught in the branches, you may not be able to free yourself without help from a buddy. If no one else is around, you're in real trouble. This may sound funny, but it actually causes unnecessary deaths.

Here are some tips for forest rides:

> Always ski or ride with reliable buddies, and never alone. Maintain constant visual or voice contact with your companions. Yodeling works great. Or carry a whistle.
> Wear a helmet and back protector.
> Go slow and stay in control.

> > Remember: Straight glades are usually avalanche paths! And surface hoar often gets buried in the forest!

A crown fracture line in a forest. Light timber does not protect from avalanches.

Freeriding in the Backcountry

When all the slopes get tracked in a ski area, many freeriders venture into the backcountry. It would be a terrible and potentially deadly mistake to assume that these rarely frequented backcountry slopes are as stable as those at a ski area, where you may often see people riding the steepest slopes in two feet (half a meter) of new snow without triggering a slide. On a ski area's slopes, frequent riding and regular avalanche control measures with explosives stabilize the snowpack. In the backcountry, however, neither is the case. At a ski area, if new snow falls on a popular freeride slope, existing tracks anchor the snowpack and reduce avalanche danger. In the backcountry, you need

⊕Martin Engler△ Allgäu, Germany

a lot of avalanche snow-how and experience (or just luck) to survive a day riding in that amount of new snow.

Though we know a lot of backcountry freeriders who would never set foot in a ski area, we recommend that less experienced riders occasionally take advantage of them to practice their skills. Don't forget that in the backcountry, you often get only a single run of maybe 3,000 vertical feet (1,000 vertical meters), often on easy-to-ride, perfect powder. Since good technique and routine are even more important in the backcountry, where you have to rely on yourself and your companions if something goes wrong, it is a good idea to get plenty of practice on ski trails.

> **Rarely frequented slopes can be dangerous even when popular off-trail slopes are still fairly safe under the same conditions.**

: Terrain analysis = applied avalanche safety

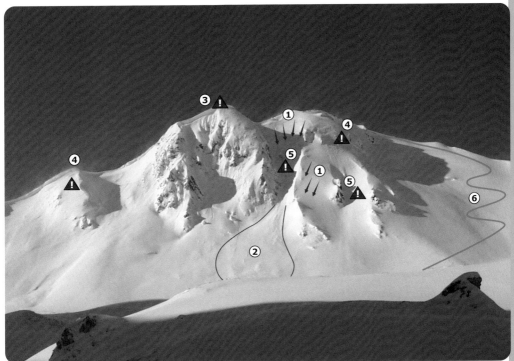

Demanding freeride area in the backcountry   ☞Patrik Nairz, Tyrolean Avalanche Warning Service

Terrain Analysis

Danger clues:

1. Old fracture lines
2. Debris deposited in the runout zone (indicates recent avalanche activity)
3. Cornices (lee slope)
4. Snow plumes blowing off ridges (blowing snow and wind loading)
5. Avalanche Gullies

Tour Planning

> Tour preparation: map, avalanche bulletin, weather report
> Assessing the situation on site

 danger zones

 old fracture line

6. Ascent route

>> Where are the descent routes?

: Earn Your Turns—Hiking

Short hikes of sometimes less than a few minutes can often provide access to powder several days after a dump. Be careful not to hike right into an avalanche slope. If you keep your eyes open and follow these basic guidelines, you'll be able to find the right route in most cases:

> The most direct line is rarely the fastest, and often the most dangerous.
> Ridges and crests usually offer the safest travel routes. Avalanches rarely release right on them, and tend to flow around them.
> Avoid steep, uniform slopes.
> Check who and what is above and below you.
> Windward (upwind) slopes are safer than leeward (downwind) slopes, which are prone to wind loading.
> On south-facing slopes, the snowpack is generally shallower and more stable than on north-facing slopes. South aspects are therefore safer and less strenuous to ascend.
> Always keep a safety distance of 15 to 20 yards between skiers or riders when traversing steep slopes.
> Always keep a very large safety distance when crossing a suspect slope, or even better, go one at a time and watch each other. If the whole party is buried, there is no one left to dig you out of the snow.
> Be particularly careful on corniced ridges, and don't get too close to the cornice roof. It can be hard to see how far out on the roof you are. Apart from the danger of falling off the ridge, the cornice might break under your weight and drag you down (see page 27).
> Keep your eyes open for sastrugi, windblown snow, cornices, ice fields, rocks and other features. The information you gather will be useful for the downhill ride.
> If possible, use telescopic poles. They make hiking easier, and reduce the risk of a fall.
> Check your equipment at the foot of the hill. If you have to get something in or out of your pack, do it there before you start climbing. It is difficult and dangerous to fiddle around with your gear in the middle of a steep slope.

A powder-rich reward for a strenuous ascent: Last ride in the late-day light.

Richard Walch △ Arlberg, Austria Patrick Wesch

> ### Hiking with Snowshoes

When hiking with snowshoes, follow the same basic rules for route finding and safe travel. Ascending with snowshoes can be fantastic, beautiful, relaxing and rewarding, but it requires good physical fitness, especially if you carry a heavy pack. Pleasure can soon turn to frustration, particularly if you are under time pressure to reach your target.

Snowshoes are not very effective on steep terrain. On slopes steeper than 30 degrees, all the fun is gone. If you use snowshoes, you'll find that traversing steep slopes is possible only in soft snow; in hard snow conditions (e.g., on morning crust), you'll have no alternative but to scramble up the fall line. Therefore it is crucial to pick a good route for hiking with snowshoes. Try to stay on relatively flat terrain to reduce risks and fatigue to a minimum.

A tranquil ascent with snowshoes

⊕Richard Walch △ Arlberg, Austria

> ### Ascending with Skis / Approach Skis

Touring skis, telemark skis, split boards and short approach skis are clearly superior to snowshoes for uphill travel. Skis offer a variety of advantages over snowshoes. Because skis can be taken up sidehills and along switchbacks, they allow efficient travel in steep terrain and extreme conditions. Their long steel edges assure good grip in conditions that send snowshoers straight back to the bottom of the hill. On skis, you can glide along flat terrain and down little hills, while snowshoers puff along and turn green with envy and fatigue. Skis allow relatively fast travel over large distances.

No matter whether you choose skis, snowshoes or plain boots, an experienced backcountry rider is easy to recognize by his or her well-selected ascent route.

> **Falls**

If you slip or fall while ascending a slope, quickly try to bring your body to a raised push-up position with your head facing uphill and your legs spread for stability. This position with your belly to the slope allows you to apply pressure with your hands and feet to slow down and control the fall. Make sure you react quickly. Don't let fear stiffen your body during the fall. It is vital to react in time before you reach a critical speed.

If you fall with your snowboard or skis strapped to your feet, the steel edges are your best chance to regain control. The strategy for slowing down after a fall is similar. Bring your head up, feet down, your board or skis perpendicular to the fall line and apply controlled pressure to the edge(s).

Many freeride courses now incorporate falling techniques in their curricula.

The Freeride Seasons

Freeriding in Early and Mid Winter

If you go freeriding around Christmas, you'll have to put up with poor conditions in most areas. Due to low temperatures and often low snow accumulations, the snowpack tends to be unstable. On the other hand, fallen powder probably will stay fluffy.

Low temperatures and a shallow snowpack lead to faceting and the increased formation of sugar snow. This process makes many slopes unstable, particularly north aspects. Rocks and other snowboard and ski killers are covered in just enough snow to become invisible, so that the equipment industry often benefits more from those powder rides than the rider does. Days are short, so ski areas close early. If conditions allow trips to the backcountry, you need good timing to get back early or you'll find yourself groping about in the dark (a headlamp can be useful).

Many riders end their midwinter freeride sessions drowning their sorrows in a resort bar. The motto is: Don't give up hope, better days will come.

Late Winter

The best conditions for freeriding are often found from mid February until the end of March. The temperature gradient between the ground and the snow surface is considerably smaller, which reduces the formation of faceted snow. The snowpack is generally deeper and more stable. If you haven't wrecked your board yet or have already gotten a new one, you can fully enjoy the regular powder dumps. The days are getting longer, leaving you with more time for backcountry touring. On the other hand, the late-winter sun quickly turns the snow soggy and burns your face if you forget your sunblock.

>> This is the best time for freeriders. Seize the day!

Perfect conditions in late winter.

⬧Richard Walch ⚡Nici Pederzolli

Spring

Spring is the favorite season of many riders and skiers, and not without a reason. Days are long and sunny; there is usually plenty of snow and considerably less competition over those generous amounts of new snow that are still falling from time to time. While this season makes flowers pop up in the lowlands and does strange things to human beings, spring is the time when the snowpack in the mountains reaches its highest levels of year. But every winter must come to an end eventually, and the intense sunshine turns the snowpack into an increasingly wet and heavy mess. Spring is the peak season for ski touring and backcountry riding, but also for wet-snow avalanches that pull the white veil from the mountains. Wet-snow avalanches, therefore, are an important factor to consider in your planning, and you have to adapt your riding habits to the peculiarities of spring conditions.

On clear nights, the snow surface regularly freezes and forms a crust. As long as you don't break that crust, the avalanche hazard usually remains low. Unfortunately, crust does not provide very good riding. It makes sense to start the day with a hike and leave time for the surface to thaw.

Strong solar radiation during the day quickly softens the snow and turns it into spring or corn snow. Riding is great until it gets too warm and the snow becomes rotten. The snowpack is often soaked to the bottom, very slow to ride and so slushy that if you try to walk on it, you're post-holing. This is the snowpack's way of saying unmistakably that the avalanche hazard has become too high, and that the freerider had better call it a day. You can always head for a last few rides on the ski trails or build a kicker in a safe spot to get a little air.

This hazard cycle through the day is typical of springtime. The avalanche danger may start at Low in the morning and pass through all the levels until it reaches High in the afternoon. Danger usually comes along with the sun. The first slopes to become dangerous are east aspects, as they receive strong radiation early in the day. South aspects are exposed to the sun for the longest period of time and become particularly water-saturated and dangerous.

West-facing slopes become the most dangerous in the evening, when the solar radiation is strongest, and shortly after sunset. Even after sunset, when the snow cover already begins to refreeze superficially, wet-snow avalanches may release. Unlike in mid winter, north-facing slopes may be more stable in springtime if the snowpack is not completely wet.

> > On water-saturated snowpacks, avalanches may release in fairly flat terrain (less than 30 degrees).

These are general guidelines for freeriding in spring. Since avalanches often break the rules, these guidelines are no easy recipe. If during the night, for instance, it rains or clouds up, the snowpack may not refreeze and stabilize. Without a crust that supports your weight, the avalanche danger may already be substantial in the morning.

Backcountry touring and longer hikes in the spring are for early-risers only. Sometimes you will have to set off before sunrise and return before noon—or the risk of ending up in a wet-snow avalanche becomes simply too high. If new snow falls in the spring, the sun turns it into a soggy mass that bonds poorly with old snow and creates widespread danger.

Richard Walch △ New Zealand Martin Rutz

: The Sun—Fun Factor and Spoilsport

Depending on the season and on snow quality, freeriders either seek the sun or try to avoid it. While the sun makes a mess of precious powder in deep winter, it also turns nasty crust into gorgeous corn snow in springtime.

Steep shady slopes are a dream for powder sessions, because the snow remains fluffy for a long time. Unfortunately these slopes are also a nightmare as far as avalanche danger is concerned. Under favorable conditions, however, northeast, north and northwest aspects offer the best chances for perfect runs, as long as you avoid the sun like a vampire. If you understand the effect of aspect and sunshine and take advantage of terrain features that protect the precious white stuff from destructive radiation, you should be able to find some powder long after the last dump. In late winter and spring, the sun is often a freerider's best friend, as it is not only good for a great tan but also transforms crust into spring snow.

For good freeriding in spring, just follow the sun. Its radiation makes all the difference between great corn snow and nasty crust and ice. East-facing slopes are the first to soften and provide good riding and skiing. On its course from the east through the south to the west, the sun transforms conditions in the same order, from east to south to west and finally north aspects. Conditions on these slopes go through various stages, from nearly impossible-to-ride ice and crust to enjoyable spring snow. But beware of excessive warming that creates rotten snow and **avalanche hazard!**

Heavily clouded skies, on the other, reduce radiation intensity and may prevent softening of the snowpack. A frozen snowpack is no fun and may be dangerous in case of a fall. When the sun shines through a thin veil of clouds, however, almost all its energy reaches the snow surface. The snow reflects this energy, and if the sky were clear, the reflected heat would disappear into space. Under a thin cloud cover, however, this long-wave radiation cannot escape and is reflected back to the surface. The result is a small localized greenhouse effect similar to the greenhouse effect that threatens our sport through global warming.

Thin cloud cover – warming in all aspects! High-energy, short-wave radiation from the sun can penetrate a thin cloud cover. The snowpack reflects a major part of this radiation and thus emits "energy." This heat energy is absorbed by clouds or fog and (mostly) reflected back to the surface resulting in a greenhouse effect – energy in the form of radiation enters the system and is not released back into space. This situation leads to warming of the snowpack in all aspects independent of how much direct solar radiation a slope receives.

Warning! This effect has an important influence on avalanche danger, since north-facing slopes now receive almost the same heat input as sunny slopes. On thinly clouded days, the snowpack rapidly heats up in all aspects, and avalanche danger may rise drastically.

: Maps—Tour Planning and Orientation

Reading maps is an important skill that is easy to learn with a little patience and discipline. Maps contain a lot of useful information and are fun to use. A glance at a map often provides a better understanding of terrain than actually traveling through it. Studying the terrain on a map is excellent preparation for backcountry touring and can often help you avoid unpleasant surprises.

Therefore, maps are indispensable tools for tour planning. Even for out-of-bounds skiing and riding around ski areas, maps are very useful. When you're on top of a slope and can't see how it ends below, just have a look at the map. The only alternative is to stick to the "earn-your-turns" motto and hike back up if you get to the bottom and can't get any farther. A map helps you locate the best spots and avoid dangerous terrain. It even allows you to look through the snowpack by providing information on the ground surface underneath. That way you can identify snow-covered glaciers with dangerous crevasses.

In springtime this information can help you identify avalanche risks like grass, which is a perfect gliding surface for wet snow. In shallow midwinter snowpacks, a map helps you to recognize dangerous rocks under a tempting layer of powder and may spare you the expense of a new board or skis or a set of new teeth. In poor visibility, the map provides much more information than your eyes. Even though it is just a piece of paper, a good map can sometimes save your life!

Basics

Freeriders use topographic maps that are scaled-down representations of the earth's surface. Maps are made to various scales, usually expressed in ratios. The larger the scale (i.e., the smaller the second number in the ratio), the more detailed the information on the map. In Europe, most freeriders and ski mountaineers use maps with a scale of 1:25,000. In the United States, many use maps with a scale of 1:24,000 (a scale commonly used on maps published by the U.S. Geological Survey), which means that one unit on the map equals 24,000 units on the surface. On a 1:24,000 map, therefore, one inch on the map equals 24,000 inches, or 2,000 feet, on the actual landscape.

Another scale commonly found on U.S. topo maps is 1:62,500, in which an inch on the map is almost exactly one mile on the ground.

Maps with a small scale (smaller than 1:50,000) provide a good overview of a wider area, but they are not suitable for tour planning because a lot of information is omitted on them (otherwise they would become too difficult to read). Maps are generalized representations of nature and use symbols to represent terrain features. Therefore each map contains a legend that explains the symbols used on it.

Compass and declination

A compass is a very cool unit: Its needle actually aligns itself with the earth's magnetic field. It will, if left horizontal and away from iron, avalanche beacons or power lines, always point to the magnetic North Pole. Unfortunately, that is different from the geographic North Pole. The difference in direction between the two is called declination. It is always indicated in the legend of your map. Good compasses will allow you to adjust to the declination of the map you're on. Don't neglect that: In western and northern areas, the declination can be more than 30 degrees.

Compass Directions

The edge of a map always runs from north to south. North is on top, and south on the bottom of the map; east is to the right, and west is on the left. Names of places are written from west to east. Many maps have a system of coordinates, or a search grid. This grid allows you to determine an exact position on the map, which can be of great importance (e.g., if you have to give your position to a helicopter pilot).

Steepness and Terrain Features

Terrain features (relief) are symbolized by contour lines. Contours are imaginary lines that join points of equal elevation on the surface of the land. Detailed maps have contour lines at intervals of 40 feet (or 20 meters), which means that each contour line represents an elevation increment of 40 feet (or 20 meters). The closer the lines are together, the steeper the terrain. If they are spaced wide apart on the map, the terrain is flat. Missing contour lines indicate plains. Every fourth or fifth line will look thicker on the map and may be labeled with the elevation above sea level (often every 500 feet or 200 meters). By using a special ruler (make sure you use the correct scale!), you can determine a slope's steepness fairly accurately without knowing the actual terrain.

Remember that the generalized representations of a map can never contain all the details.

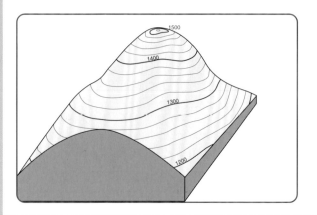

A peak is represented by contour lines on a topographic map. It takes some imagination to get a three-dimensional picture from a map.

(not to scale)

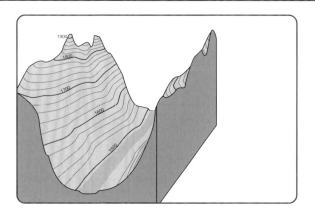

Water always flows on the bottom of valleys. Terrain rises on both sides of rivers, creeks and other drainage paths.

> >

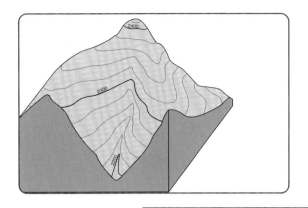

If you can correctly interpret contour lines on a map, you'll be able to identify critical sections in a tour or ride in advance.

(not to scale)

Cliff bands and drop-offs with a height of less than 100 feet may be too small to be captured by the map, but too high for you to jump down. The overall shape of the terrain, except for minor details, is represented by contour lines. Interpreting this two-dimensional representation of three-dimensional reality may be a bit difficult at first and requires a little practice.

Maps provide vital information on terrain (relief) that allows you to identify crucial sections (such as steep open slopes) in advance and adapt your route to them. Similarly, this information can be used for finding suitable ascent and descent routes according to prevailing conditions.

Working with Maps

Maps are indispensable tools for planning tours. (See the map on the following two pages.) In addition to a map, you'll need a pencil and a simple magnifying glass (makes reading easier), a ruler for measuring slope inclination and, if available, a guidebook of the relevant area.

Orienting the Map

Orienting the map means bringing it into a position in which north on the map is in line with true north. This is easy to do by using a compass adjusted to your present declination or by identifying land features such as rivers, roads or ski lifts. Once you've adjusted your compass to the degree of declination indicated on the map, align the baseplate of the compass with the edge of the map, and rotate the map with the compass until the north end of the magnetic needle is in line with the N mark on the compass housing.

The map is now oriented and all the information on it corresponds to the terrain in front of you.

Determining Your Position

Before you set off, you have to determine the position of the trailhead. This is easy to do with the help of landmarks such as trailheads, rivers and the end of a road. Advanced techniques can be used to determine your position if there are no suitable landmarks (e.g., on a high plain in winter). Please refer to specialized literature if you are interested in these techniques, because we will not discuss them in this chapter.

CONTOURS

Contour lines

Contour line at 7000 ft

checked spot elevation

GLACIERS AND PERMANENT SNOWFIELDS

Contours and limits

Form lines

SURFACE FEATURES

Levee

Intricate surface area

Gravel beach or glacial moraine

Sand or mud area, dunes, or shifting sand

VEGETATION

Woods

Scrub

RIVERS, LAKES, AND CANALS

Intermittent stream

Intermittent river

Disappearing Stream

Perennial river

Small falls; small rapids

large falls; large rapids

Masonary dam

Dam with lock

Dam carrying road

Perennial lake; Intermittent lake or pond

Dry lake

Narrow wash

Wide wash

Well or spring, spring or seep

BUILDINGS AND RELATED FEATURES

Buildings

Airport

Landing strip

ROADS AND RELATED FEATURES

Light duty road

Unimproved road

Trail

Bridge

Drawbridge

Tunnel

BOUNDARIES

Park, reservation, or monument

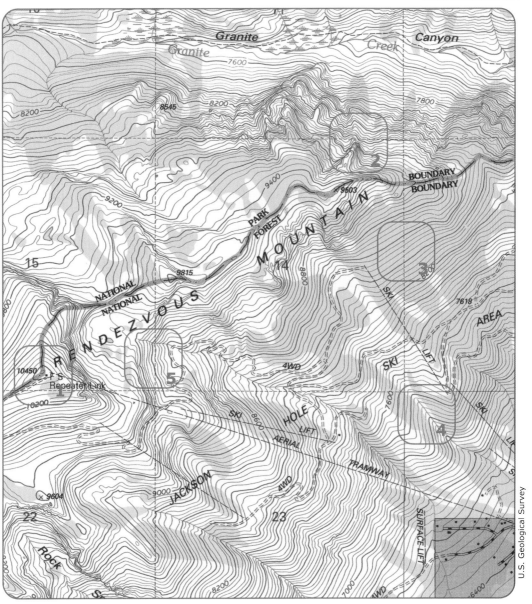

Scale: 1:24.000

U.S. Geological Survey

 Summit

 Cliffs

 Intermediate steep slope (forest)

 Gully

 Extremely steep area

How to Determine Your Starting Point and Destination

The first step is to use your map to determine where you want to set off and where you want to end up on the tour you are planning. Then you use all your snow-how and mountain knowledge to draw the best route from your starting point to your destination. If you don't have the necessary knowledge and experience, consider hiring a mountain guide or team up with more experienced riders. Identify critical sections along the route and avoid particularly dangerous areas. Make sure that your route is not too long and demanding. Give preference to relatively flat and steady ascents.

Slope steepness is an important criterion for ascent and descent routes. Plan possible alternatives and escape routes. Have an alternative destination planned in case adverse conditions make it impossible to ride or ski any critical sections or dangerous slopes along your original route. That way you can still enjoy your trip and don't have to give it up altogether.

How to Determine Slope Angle on Map

Special rulers (usually made of transparent plastic with a scale along the edge for measuring slope angle) are available to facilitate this task. This is how you use them:

1. Locate the slope section that you want to measure on the map.
2. Align the ruler perpendicular to the contour lines.
3. Make sure that the increments on the scale correspond with those of the contour lines.
4. Take the steepest reading (where the contour lines are closest together), and add one degree of inclination to make sure you don't underestimate slope angle. That way you have an extra safety margin.
5. The result is the approximate slope inclination. (Note that the actual inclination may be steeper due to wind loading or inaccurate maps.)

How to Determine Slope Aspect

Determining slope aspect on a map is crucial for planning backcountry tours (also be sure to consult the current avalanche bulletin). The contour lines help you to determine a slope's orientation. Draw a line along the parallel contour lines of a slope and then a line perpendicular to the parallel one: that's the fall line. Finally, compare this direction with north on the map to find out this slope's aspect. Note that a single slope may have several aspects.

Tour Preparation and Time Management

Apart from steepness, the length of an ascent is the most important factor for estimating the amount of time you require. The distance you travel is a crucial factor for time management. Use a ruler to measure the approximate distance on the map and calculate the real distance according to the scale of your map.

At a scale of 1:62,500, 1 inch on the map equals 1 mile in nature. At a scale of 1:50,000, 1 cm on the map equals 500 meters on the ground.

"The death of a mountaineer is always a tragic accident as it ends the life of a person who did not seek death but a deeper sense of being alive."

Ruedi Schatz

Famous for his extra-smooth riding style, American snowboarding icon Jeff Curtes Craig Kelly Craig Kelly won four World Freestyle Championships and three U.S. Open Championships before turning his attention to backcountry freeriding and developing products for Burton. He was tragically killed in an avalanche in the Selkirk Mountains of British Columbia in late January 2003, along with six others.

Rules of Thumb for Calculating the Required Time:

Expect to travel at approximate rate of...

> 2.5 miles (4.0 km) per hour for the horizontal distance traveled when using skis, or 2.0 miles (3.2 km) per hour using snowshoes, plus...

> 1,000 feet (300 m) per hour for vertical distance climbed when using skis, or probably 800 feet (250 m) per hour when using snowshoes.

Remember that skis allow you to travel much faster! Calculate your total amount of required time by adding the time for vertical distance to the time for horizontal distance. The amount of time required depends to a large degree on snow and terrain conditions, as well as on your personal fitness. These are only very rough guidelines. Always allow some extra time for the unexpected.

Example of a Tour

>> 3 miles (5 km) for the horizontal distance = approx. 1 hour
>> 2,000 feet (600 m) for the vertical distance = roughly 2 hours
Total amount of time required:
>> Distance = 1 hour
>> Ascent = 2 hours
Total = 3 hours
Total amount of time required for the ascent is approximately three hours.

This timeframe includes a margin for unexpected difficulties (such as broken equipment or detours to avoid dangerous sections), but not for extended breaks. Good planning always provides for some extra time. You will also have to determine the latest time to return regardless of whether or not you have reached your destination. In the spring you will have to set this time fairly early or you risk getting caught in a wet-snow slide. If the avalanche danger rises during the day (e.g., in the spring), it is vital that you set off early enough. An early start is also the rule for long tours.

The decision whether it is possible to go on a certain tour or ride a given slope depends on current snow and weather conditions. (See also the "The Avalanche Bulletin" and "The 3x3 Filter Method" sections in Chapter 3.) It is critical that you carefully assess all risk factors before setting off. When choosing a tour, first examine all relevant slope angles and aspects and decide whether this trip is possible under current conditions.

Guidebooks

Guidebooks provide good information for longer excursions into the backcountry. Though most of these books were written for hikers, they are a valuable source of information for all backcountry travelers. Guidebooks may provide information on routes, terrain, huts, important phone numbers and other topics. However, no guidebook can ever replace your independent evaluation of the avalanche danger.

Chapter 7

: Info: Avalanche Control, The Environment, Snowmobiling, Responsibility

⊡Dan Ferrer △ Chamonix, France ⅙ Seb Michaud

: Freeriding and the Environment

Our mountains are a paradise for freeriders, but they are also the habitat of many endangered animal and plant species. The glaciers and mountain lakes provide us with drinking water, and in remote Alpine environments, many a Swiss mountain farmer grows his well-known "herbal remedies" (for recreational use). The more remote ranges are often the last remaining habitats for grizzly bears, caribou and other animals. Nonetheless we are sawing on the branch we are sitting on. Excessive consumption of fossil fuels has led to global warming and caused a significant rise in temperatures. Statistical data proves that our winters are continually getting warmer, and in many places the lack of snow threatens recreational activities. The dry winters of recent years give us a taste of the possible future of our sport. Freeriding without powder is like a party without music, drinks and guests! Even though some people still don't seem to be willing to accept the facts (probably not until the last glacier of North America has disappeared), each of us should make some sort of contribution to reduce the damage. Let us do what we can, and hope for the best!

Fauna

The mountains are full of animals, even if we usually don't get to see any more of them than the tracks they leave behind. Alpine species are well adapted to the harsh conditions of their habitat, but they do not tolerate human interference all that well. Winter is a particularly difficult period for these animals, and scarce food supplies force them to limit their energy consumption. If we disturb their winter rest and scare them, we threaten their lives.

The Forest

Forests play a crucial role in alpine environments. Forests reduce avalanche danger, and protect from falling rocks and landslides. With their ability to retain large amounts of water, forests also have a function in flood control. Forests are particularly important at timberline for preventing the release of avalanches. In harsh alpine climates, trees grow much slower than those farther down in the valleys. The growth rate is sometimes only six or seven feet in 100 years. These trees constantly struggle for survival and are very sensitive to the slightest damage. In the densely populated European Alps, freeriding in forests is illegal, as the forests are needed to protect mountain villages from avalanches. In North America, we are free to use the forests (if they are public), but we need to respect them.

Flora

Plants are at the bottom of the food chain in alpine environments. Dense vegetation also prevents erosion and helps control land and rock slides. The vegetative cover on ski trails is often severely damaged and only partially fulfills its ecological function.

These thoughtless people don't realize they are destroying vegetation, which could lead to serious erosion.

⌨Sebi Perach △ Val d'Isère, France

> **Waste**

The short summers of mountain zones leave hardly enough time for garbage to decompose. In extreme cases, refuse may remain for hundreds of years in the spot where it was disposed. Aluminum cans, water bottles and other plastics, cigarette butts and other trash have a long-term impact on the environment.

> **Snowmobiling and Respecting Nature**

Riding a snowmobile is fun, a lot of fun actually. In remote areas of North America, these vehicles are often the only choice for travel over large distances in the backcountry. Admittedly, snowmobiles can be very useful for this purpose. However, problems arise from riding snowmobiles as a sport. High-marking in national forests (and other mountain areas) shows the same degree of ignorance as throwing a stick of dynamite into a mountain stream. The impact on local fauna is dramatic, and the consequences can be deadly for endangered species. (Modern snowmobiles can also be hard on snowboarders and skiers. Their tracks in the snow can set up hard and can be a nasty surprise.)

We would like to encourage you to use snowmobiles only as means of transportation for reaching remote areas.

It's your choice!

Anybody who goes freeriding has a negative influence on the environment. One of the largest problems is traffic. Public transportation is often not available or considered too inconvenient. Snowcats and helicopters burn countless gallons of fuel, the energy consumption of ski lifts is equally huge, and ski area operators keep expanding facilities into previously inaccessible areas that require more and more energy use.

The damage that's already done, however, can mostly be fixed. It is very much worth our time to protect our mountain environments. In order to permit freeriding for generations to come, we should try to reduce our impact to a minimum. Each and every one of us can contribute his or her share without a lot of effort and without having to give up anything.

Just stick to the following guidelines:

> **Take all your garbage back to the valley.**
> **Respect trees and plants.**
> **Avoid runs and sections through shallow snow. If there is no alternative, take off your skis or snowboard and walk, otherwise you'll risk damaging scarce food supplies for wildlife and the plants that protect slopes from erosion and landslides.**
> **Stay away from young trees and reforestation areas. The sharp steel edges of your skis or snowboard destroy the sensitive little trees.**
> **If you see any wildlife, enjoy the sight. Then go around them, keeping your distance, or choose a different route.**
> **Cigarette butts contaminate water and take many years to decompose, so take them with you.**
> **If possible leave your car at home, and try to load the vehicles you use with as many passengers as you can. That way you can help reduce emissions of the greenhouse gas carbon dioxide and save money.**
> **Take advantage of bus services provided in ski areas.**
> **Don't ride snowmobiles just for fun through the backcountry.**

The Fight Against Avalanches

Prolonged intense snowfalls as they occurred in the winter of 1998–99 in Europe can lead to extreme avalanche hazard and threaten roads and human settlements. In such disaster situations, the responsible authorities have the power and the duty to close entire valleys until the situation returns to normal. In ski resorts, explosives are used to artificially release slides and control the danger.

Engineering Works

Deflectors are walls that intercept avalanches or redirect their flow. Retarders are obstacles in avalanche paths designed to slow down the slide's speed and reduce its destructive potential.

Roads and railways are sometimes protected by snow sheds and tunnels to avoid the necessity of temporary closures. All of these artificial structures are extremely costly and interfere with delicate alpine environments.

Horizontal ledges in starting zones to prevent avalanche release. In the catastrophic winter of 1998–99 massive snowfalls buried even very large defensive structures. As a result these structures sometimes could no longer prevent the release of avalanches (as shown in this image).
☞ Swiss Federal Institute for Snow and Avalanche Research, FISAR

Avalanche Control Measures by Explosives

The objective of these measures is to release avalanches under controlled conditions before the potential threat becomes large enough to cause damage or claim victims. The slides are released by explosive charges tossed by ski patrollers, launched by surplus military artillery or pneumatic cannons or dropped from helicopters. In easily accessible areas, hand charges may be directly thrown or placed in the blasting location. Pneumatic cannons (Avalauncher) and bomb trams are clearly visible in some ski areas and indicate frequent control measures in these slopes.

Warning signs and closed runs indicate temporary closure for avalanche hazard and control measures.

After snowfalls control measures with explosives take place at most ski areas.

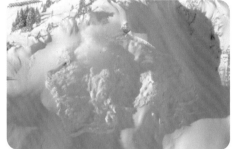

⊕Tobias Hafele △ Arlberg, Austria

Forests for Permanent Avalanche Protection

More than a thousand years ago the mountain dwellers of Europe recognized the importance of forests for avalanche control. In the 14th century what remained of mountain forests were put under protection and their exploitation was banned in order to preserve them because excessive cutting had brought death and destruction to the people by avalanches.

Forests decelerate wind, reduce wind loading and thus avoid the formation of very large avalanches. However, trees cannot stop dangerous slab avalanches.

Unfortunately many forests have been logged into moonscapes or severely damaged by acid rain or insect infestations, all of which reduces their protective function. The huge powder avalanches that occurred in Europe in the catastrophic winter of 1998–99 destroyed entire forests and reduced them to piles of debris.

Avalanche Accidents, the Law and Personal Responsibility

Despite good planning and sensible conduct, you can **never** fully exclude the possibility that an accident **will happen**. If one does happen, it's a terrible situation for everyone involved. Apart from feelings of guilt, a slide creates worry about injured friends and causes sorrow from deaths.

If any individual is injured or killed in an avalanche, the authorities investigate the causes of the accident. If anyone can be held responsible, it is up to the authorities to decide whether a law has been broken. In the presence of suspicious circumstances, legal proceedings will be taken to clarify the matter. Since legal situations differ from country to country and even between individual states, we will give you only an overview of relevant issues.

⊙Bavarian Avalanche Warning Service △ Berchtesgaden, Germany

Deadly human-released avalanche in a north facing slope with an inclination of "only" 30° at an elevation of 1900 m above sea level. Fracture line in the area of trees and rocks. A ski tourer released this approximately 75 cm thick and "only" 15 m wide slab at High Hazard. Though S&R was called immediately, the skier could not be rescued alive.

Basics

Every freerider is expected to gather information from the avalanche bulletin (if available) before leaving patrolled ski trails. This simple precaution is a must! Anyone who does not make this simple precaution is negligent. The same is true if a rider or skier ignores restricted areas or warning signs that indicate dangerous out-of-bounds areas. If such behavior leads to an avalanche accident, the individual may be guilty of negligence and suffer the legal consequences of such an offence.

You can often see freeriders riding slopes directly above ski trails with unsuspecting skiers below them. If an avalanche is triggered in such a place, it may injure or even kill innocent individuals. Don't be surprised if the ski patrol confiscates your ski pass if you are caught causing danger for individuals on the trails below. If you should trigger a slide that injures someone below, you could suffer the legal consequences.

It is up to you to decide how much risk you want to take. The 3x3 Filter Method and the Reduction Method provide a good tool for calculating the acceptable risk. As long as you stay within the safety margin provided by these methods, you will most likely never be held responsible for an accident.

Shared Risk

Most freeriders who travel together in the backcountry share a more or less equal degree of experience and knowledge. In this situation everyone in the group is respon-sible for his or her companions, but in case of an accident, it is unlikely that anyone will be held responsible, since everyone knew the risk and incurred it voluntarily.

The situation becomes more difficult if one person in the group takes the lead. Then decisions are no longer made democratically, and the remaining group members follow the decisions of the leader. These so-called leaders often don't have the necessary skills, and become leaders only because of their athletic prowess (real or imagined), their willingness to accept a higher risk and their natural inclination to be the top dog. Don't blindly follow a supposedly better and more experienced rider. Make your own decisions and act responsibly and independently. Discuss possible risks and presumably wrong or right decisions in the group. Nobody is perfect, and your life is at stake!

De Facto Leaders

De facto leaders are individuals such as snowboard or ski instructors who guide friends or other persons on excursions on the basis of their professional skills and experiences. Their companions assume that they are safe with their guide. The de facto leader's com-petence is rarely questioned, which is often flattering and encourages them to take higher risks. Generally the group member with the highest degree of snow-how and experience and the best specific training is responsible for his companions.

This doesn't mean that if you have taken an avalanche course, you should no longer go on a tour with less experienced friends because you may be held responsible if something goes wrong. One solution is to agree to make all decisions together, and that each and everyone takes responsibility for his or her own acts.

Guided Tours

If you go on a guided tour, participate in a freeride camp or hire a mountain guide for a backcountry tour, you entrust yourself to a specially trained professional who is responsible for your safety. However, mountain guides can never promise their clients 100 percent safety because, as we all know, there is no such thing in the mountains. The guide must always inform the client of existing risks.

In the case of an accident, the mountain guide will be held responsible and the authorities will investigate the case to find out whether there are any grounds for legal proceedings.

Independent of the legal situation you should always think twice about whom you go riding with or whom you bring along on a tour. Your companions' competence and equipment are your life insurance. Many riders are great in the pipe, the fun park or at the snow bar, but freeriding requires different qualities, such as responsibility, risk awareness, reliability, competence, snow-how and intuition.

False Idols

Freeride movies and magazines show how riders crank their turns on extremely steep slopes and take risky jumps over cornices and cliffs. These professional riders look like stunt men, and that is exactly what they are. What you don't see in these movies are all the technical backup and extensive preparations required to make these shots. Riders are in touch with safety experts and helicopter pilots who warn them of slides through radio communication systems. If a rider is in a dead-end situation, he can be evacuated by helicopter. Despite of all these safety precautions involving large teams of specialists, riders still take a high risk. Don't forget that these freeriders are professionals who often ride and ski the whole year round. Though many pros have a high degree of experience, some of them are greenhorns who don't know much about avalanche danger. Today, more and more professional riders get special training to improve their snow-how.

The extreme runs you can see in freeride movies are usually shot in coastal Alaska and Canada, never in the interior mountains of North America or the mountains of Europe, where riding such slopes would be suicide! Everybody involved in these productions knows that; only the viewers don't. The snowpack in Alaska is often stable enough to allow riding under these extreme conditions. Nevertheless, riders and film crews often spend weeks waiting for a single perfect day to shoot a few runs.

Other questionable idols include ski and snowboard **instructors**. The avalanche knowledge of these so-called experts is often **completely insufficient**, though there are always exceptions. Many accidents are caused by instructors because avalanches don't care whether their victims are so-called experts or not. Therefore, your best option is to get the necessary snow-how that allows you to assess the situation independently and make your own decisions.

>> Be cool, stay yourself...

>>

>> A spectacular stunt: Noah Brandon has been a professional freerider for 13 years and knows what he is doing!
Richard Walch ▲ New Zealand Noah Brandon

: Snowmobiling and Avalanche Danger

In North America, unlike in Europe, snowmobiling is very popular and common. Free-riders, would-be sportsmen and residents of remote areas use snowmobiles for transportation (often there is no other available means) or simply for the fun of riding them.

With a little practice, anyone can ride even extreme terrain on a modern high-tech snowmobile. Their vehicles allow snowmobile riders to penetrate further into the backcountry within a single day than backcountry skiers or snowboarders could travel in an entire week. Snowmobiles undeniably offer a variety of advantages, but there is also a darker side to them. A rising number of avalanche accidents are caused by snowmobilers. In the United States, snowmobilers already account for more than a quarter of all avalanche fatalities. No other "sport" causes more avalanche accidents, and the upward trend continues.

The heavy weight of the snowmobile puts enormous stresses on the fragile snowpack. Remember that almost every steep snowcovered slope is capable of producing avalanches with large additional loads. High speed and radical maneuvers further increase stresses (and things get even worse if the snowmobiler gets his machine stuck). The additional load caused by a snowmobile is surpassed only by explosives used for control measures. The power of the engine often gives a false sense of security and causes riders to over-rate their abilities. The high speed and motor noises make it virtually impossible to notice danger signs.

The more slopes are ridden in one day, the higher the accumulated or overall risk of riding into an unstable slope and triggering a slide. This is aggravated by the large distances that can be covered by snowmobilers and the variety of terrain they often travel through in a single day. Remember that snowpack stability and avalanche hazard vary greatly in different areas and on slopes. Snowboarders and backcountry skiers have much more time to assess avalanche danger and make sensible decisions. Attentive boarders or skiers are able to recognize warning signs and changing conditions and are able to adapt quickly to them, whereas snowmobilers who ride up 40-degree slopes at 40 miles per hour are playing avalanche roulette. The chances of survival may be larger than in the Russian version of this popular game, but the risk is nevertheless so high that it can hardly be called residual risk.

: Risk Reduction for Snowmobilers?

The Reduction Method does not work for snowmobilers. Nevertheless there are some possibilities for increasing the life span of "testosterone sled riders." The 3x3 Filter Method can be used for defensive snowmobiling. You just have to keep in mind that although a snowpack may support 10 overweight skiers without starting to slide, it may not be able to take the weight of a single hillbilly high-marking on a sled. If you want to limit the risk of triggering an avalanche when riding a snowmobile, you must take the high stresses caused by your heavy vehicle into account!

Stick to the following rules:

> Stay in flat or moderately steep terrain (less than 30 degrees).

> Ride slopes steeper than 30 degrees only in very favorable conditions (Low Danger).

> Always go one at a time on steep slopes, and have your partner observe you the whole time while you're climbing.

> Always be prepared for an accident.

> Be very cautious about high-marking. More than 70 percent of all snowmobile avalanche accidents happen during high-marking.

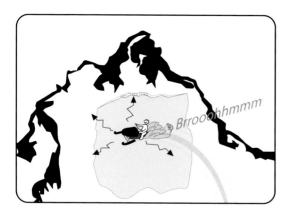

Brrooohhmmm

High-marking hillbilly racer on his testosterone sled triggering a slab avalanche ...

>>> Warning:

Snowmobiles can remotely trigger avalanches great distances away, and avalanches triggered by snowmobiles tend to be deeper and larger. Stay clear of runout zones at Considerable or higher danger levels! In our opinion, snowmobiles may be useful for extensive backcountry trips and expeditions, as well as for long approaches, but they are totally out of place in the sensitive environments of high alpine regions.

A high-brain, low-tech approach offers the best chance to enjoy a long life as a happy freerider.

Group Dynamics, Risk Perception and Avalanche Accidents

"We must not ... forget that our thoughts and our actions are influenced to a larger degree by ideals, goals, desires and motives than by logic and actual facts."

Werner Munter

The more riders or skiers on a slope, the higher the additional load and therefore the risk of triggering an avalanche. That should be pretty clear to anyone. Our brains, however, tend to trick us into believing the exact opposite! Being part of a larger group gives us a false sense of safety, even though statistical evidence proves that an extremely high number of avalanche accidents occur with large groups consisting of six to 10 individuals. Furthermore, many of these accidents were not even caused by incorrect assessment of the situation, but by wrong decisions due to group dynamics. How is that possible?

> Skiers or snowboarders who are willing to take higher risks get or maintain the respect of their group. In groups, the loudest and strongest people (so-called alpha animals or top dogs) tell the others what to do. During times of avalanche risk, this attitude may be deadly!

> Individuals who do not like (or are not able) to make their own decisions are tempted to transfer all responsibility to the group. Dominant people who like to be leaders are often more than willing to assume this responsibility. But check what their leadership is based on. Recklessness and high risk tolerance are ineffective weapons against avalanches.

> Perceptions and mental processes in a group often create a dangerous illusion of one's own infallibility. Overrating your own abilities can be deadly!

> Instead of assessing dangers in a comprehensive way, we tend to avoid thinking about possible dangers. Typical thoughts are: "It'll be alright," or "It can't happen to us."

> The false sense of security creates a tunnel vision that excludes alternatives, variations and other opinions.

> Many alpinists (and other persons) have a ballistic attitude, like a bullet that has left the gun barrel and cannot be stopped. Once they have made the decision to climb a mountain and ski down from the top, they push it through, no matter what happens. The result of this attitude is often disastrous. The personal motivation is so high that warning signs and adversities are no longer perceived. The outcome of this ballistic attitude is often catastrophic.

> Individuals who try to analyze decisions (and expectations) critically are often dismissed as whiners or sissies.

> The mere fact that no slide has been triggered yet can lure groups (but also individuals) into thinking that their conduct is correct. This is another dangerous mistake. Even if you have not triggered an avalanche, you never know how close you were to hell!

Situations that often lead to dangerous group dynamics include previous failures, situations of competition ("who is the best?" contests), groups that consist of "specialists" (everyone wants to be the "most special" of the group) and authoritarian leadership.

How to Avoid the Group Trap

Most powderhounds find it difficult, actually extremely difficult, to translate their knowledge of avalanche dangers into sensible decisions that keep their risk to a minimum. Only those who are aware of their weaknesses and limitations are able to manage their potential for incorrect assessment and dumb decision making and still make sensible decisions in critical situations.

> Ask yourself the following question before setting off: Should I go on this tour or ride this slope under these conditions with these people?

> Avoid large groups (groups consisting of more than five individuals).

> Mature freeriders don't need to impress others with reckless stunts.

> Decisions must be carried by the whole group; everybody has a right to veto a decision. Every member must be informed about the risk, and that risk should not be taken without the consent of all members. The remote and abstract concept of risk becomes more tangible and real when you have to discuss it and make provisions for emergencies.

> Learn how to make careful decisions in tense situations and under time pressure.

> Positive leadership is required to avoid critical situations and/or to make the right decisions in such situations. These qualities of positive leadership include: **natural authority, a power of persuasion, determination, social skills, team spirit and good communication, consideration toward others (without it, a person might trigger an avalanche) and the ability to improvise.**

Critically analyze your own conduct and desires during or after each tour or freeride day. Ask yourself whether your conduct and riding were appropriate and sensible for that day's conditions.

 **Nobody is perfect.**

Although we consider ourselves educated and rational beings, we are actually much less rational than we would like to admit. Independent of our personal intelligence, our brains often fail in complex situations. A high IQ is no protection from avalanches! Tunnel vision and ballistic behavior occur independent of one's intelligence. If you want to live long as a freerider, you must accept our imperfect nature as human beings. Nobody can ever be absolutely certain whether **this** particular slope is stable or whether it will produce an avalanche. Despite all of our technical and scientific progress, we are still unable to control avalanches.

> **Freeriders and freeskiers have no other choice but to**
> **> Think in terms of probability,**
> **> Develop an awareness for potential dangers, and**
> **> Accept that the forces of nature are and remain unpredictable and uncontrollable.**

Freeriders require the cognitive abilities of holistic thinking and networking in order to perceive the complex and dynamic processes that create avalanche hazard. Limiting your assessment to individual factors can lead to catastrophic errors! Avalanche hazard involves a complex physical system of causes and effects, and is additionally strongly influenced by human psychology. In order to make the right decisions in this chaos, we need a holistic network of assessment strategies (such as the 3x3 Filter Method) that forces us to collect as much information as possible and process this information correctly. At the same time, this system must be quick and simple to use so that anybody can apply it without having to invest too much time.

Apart from the methods for assessing potential risks and making the right (low-risk) decisions, freeriders also need good intuition. We must develop the ability to make the right decisions despite or even because of contradicting and incomplete information. Perception, reason and intuition are the tools that help us fulfill this difficult task.

>> Chapter 8 : Freeriding = A Sport for Those Who Use Their Heads

"Nature, to be commanded, must be obeyed."
Francis Bacon

Crevasses ⊕Richard Walch

Freeriding is a game in which the rules are always made by the mountain, never by the riders. And the mountain is free to change these the rules every day. It is up to us to recognize and understand this and keep playing along.

Good freeriding always involves gathering information and correctly evaluating that information. Apart from good technique and a feeling for your snowboard or skis, knowledge and experience are indispensable requirements for freeriding. The backcountry is not a place for those who are unwilling to deal with the dangers of winter mountain environments. If a life sentence in the fun park seems too harsh to you, and if you don't have the necessary funds to regularly hire a mountain guide, it is highly recommended that you take an avalanche course. Again, freeriding is not a sport to learn by trial and error or by a do-it-yourself method.

Many who have refused to believe this have lost their lives. Others were just lucky. But you can't rely on your luck forever. Don't hesitate to spend a few bucks on a course. If your luck runs out, you won't be able to spend your money at all.

: Avalanche Courses and Freeride Camps

Freeriding has been booming in recent years, and an ever-growing number of snow-boarders and skiers, particularly younger individuals, are lured by the boundless pleasures that wait off the beaten ski trail. Many of these riders do not observe even the most elemental rules and safety precautions. Some of them just don't care, but most simply don't know any better. Recognizing dangers requires knowledge and practical skills, and these skills must be learned in a course. Theoretical knowledge provides a good basis for getting started, but it can never replace a practical course. A course offers you the opportunity to apply your skills in the field and have somebody correct you every time you do something wrong. You don't get that chance when you are on your own, and one day you may pay dearly for a small mistake.

In recent years, there has been an increasing demand for avalanche courses. In most areas, private and public organizations now offer a variety of courses to meet this demand.

A good avalanche course should provide you with the necessary knowledge and skills to enjoy freeriding at an acceptable risk and enable you to take responsibility for your own risk management.

The wide selection of courses offered allows you to choose a curriculum that is best suited for your individual skill level. Offerings range from two-day basic courses to special weeklong freeride camps for very experienced riders. Courses are usually open to snowboarders, skiers and telemarkers. Depending on the curriculum, these courses will cover, theoretically and practically, much of the information found in this book.

Huge cornice

⌖ **Martin Engler**

A course offers you the opportunity to apply everything you have learned from this book in the field. An avalanche course is not only a good investment, it is also a lot of fun and will enhance your riding. Depending on the type of course, the curriculum may deal with such issues as:

Basic Camp:

> Types of avalanches and how they form
> Interpreting the avalanche bulletin
> Using transceivers and other emergency equipment
> Locating buried victims and companion rescue
> Measuring slope angle and determining slope aspect
> Effects of wind and weather conditions on avalanche danger
> Checking risk

Apart from these issues, an advanced freeride camp may also offer:

> Intensive training in companion rescue
> Tour planning with a map and compass
> Orientation
> Risk management through the use of the 3x3 Filter Method or similar systems
> Route finding
> Backcountry touring
> First aid in mountain environments

Special camps for experienced riders

offer the opportunity to acquire additional skills, such as:
> Rappelling and other mountaineering skills
> Using crampons and piolets
> Extreme freeriding (very steep slopes, channels and couloirs)

The most important considerations for choosing a course should be safety and the quality of training. Certified mountain guides and experienced freeride instructors guarantee a standard of excellence. More and more ski and snowboard schools now also offer avalanche courses and freeride camps. Prices and course content often vary considerably. Get as much information as possible about the qualifications of the operators and instructors before you make your choice. See also Chapter 9 for useful addresses and phone numbers. More information can be found on the Internet at **www. POWDERGUIDE .com.**

> > Save you(r) mate!

: Epilogue by Werner Munter

Dear Powder Fans,

If you are convinced that freeriding is among the most beautiful things on this planet, lend me your ear and accept some advice from an old man. Even if you normally prefer to live by your own rules, make an exception and consider these **three simple guidelines.**

1. Don't become a victim of the white rush. Distrust that tricky powder that lets you fly so high. Stay cool, and check your risk! And, lets face it, "the steeper the run, the better the fun" is bullshit. I'll bet you that you'll draw the most radical turns at around 35 degrees!

2. Be smart and adapt your riding to the conditions. The mountain is always stronger than you. Give it up, if the risk is too high (it's easy now to assess your risk), or you'll waste your life. You'll see that next year the mountain will still be there in all its glory, and you will be around as well.

3. In life-threatening situations, your belly is often more reliable than your head. When you've got that bad feeling in your gut, you know that this is not your day. Go with your gut, even if your head is trying to tell you something else and your buddies are laughing at you. It's better to be chicken and survive than to be a hero and die!

If you stick to these rules and have a little bit of luck, you can surf that powder for **many years to come.**

I believe this book will be a huge success, and I hope that all worried parents, friends and partners of passionate powder hounds will give this book as a gift.

—Werner Munter
Arolla, Switzerland,
September 2002

[aK]
RIDE SMARTER
LESS REALLY IS MORE

ARTICULATED HOOD

WATERPROOF ZIPPERS

WELDED SEAMS

VENTING CHEST POCKETS

SURE GRIP ZIP PULL

TWO-WAY CENTER FRONT ZIP

ADJUSTABLE VELCRO CUFF CLOSURE

THE AK 3L CONTINUUM FUSE JACKET

BREATH DEEP. RIDE STRONG

The AK™ Continuum Fuse Jacket signifies a major leap forward in outerwear perfection—a high-tech second skin that breathes, feels, fits, and performs like nothing else so you ride longer, smarter, and harder.

WELDED SEAMS

ORIGAMI CONSTRUCTION

WWW.BURTON.COM

Richard Walch △ Aspen Vinzenz Lüps

>> Chapter 9 : Resources

bove the clouds, on a peak with a view. ⌾Thorsten Indra △ Lebanon ⚡Sven Gittermann, Holger Feist, Lars Gittermann

www.powderguide.com — powder-fresh information for freeriders

Our service page provides regularly updated information and full service for
all powder enthusiasts.
On this website you will find the latest information about:

> Avalanches and weather
> Risk management and avalanches
> Tips for backcountry touring
> Useful addresses
> Information on transceivers and the latest innovations for freeriding
> Links to the best freeride websites
> And a lot more

: U.S. Avalanche Forecasts

>> North American Map

> ## > U.S. Avalanche Forecasts   www.avalanche.org / www.csac.org

Alaska

Southeast Alaska Avalanche Center   www.avalanche.org/~seaac

California

Central Sierra–Lake Tahoe/Donner
Summit Area (Truckee)   530-587-2158   www.r5.fs.fed.us/tahoe/avalanche.html
Eastern Sierra (Mammoth Lakes)   760-924-5500   www.csac.org/Bulletins/Calif/current.html
Mount Shasta   530-926-9613   www.shastaavalanche.org

Colorado

Statewide (Denver/Boulder)	303-275-5360	www.geosurvey.state.co.us/avalanche
Statewide (Colorado Springs)	719-520-0020	www.geosurvey.state.co.us/avalanche
Front Range (Fort Collins)	970-482-0457	www.geosurvey.state.co.us/avalanche
Summit County and Vail areas	970-668-0600	www.geosurvey.state.co.us/avalanche
Aspen area	970-920-1664	www.geosurvey.state.co.us/avalanche
San Juan Mountains (Durango)	970-247-8187	www.geosurvey.state.co.us/avalanche
Crested Butte area	970-641-7161	www.cbavalanchecenter.org

Idaho

Sun Valley	208-622-8027	www.avalanche.org/~svavctr

Montana

Northwest Montana Rockies (Whitefish)	406-257-8402	www.fs.fed.us/r1/lolo/avalanche
Central and Southwestern Rockies (Bozeman)	406-587-6981	www.mtavalanche.com
Southern Mountains (Cooke City)	406-587-6981	www.mtavalanche.com
Southern Mountains (West Yellowstone)	406-587-6981	www.mtavalanche.com

New Hampshire

Tuckerman and Huntington ravines	603-466-2713	www.tuckerman.org

Oregon

South Washington Cascades and Mount Hood (Portland)	503-808-2400	www.nwac.noaa.gov

Utah

Sundance/Mount Timpanogos area (Provo)	801-378-4333	www.avalanche.org/~uac
Park City area	435-658-5512	www.avalanche.org/~uac
Tri-Canyon area (Salt Lake City)	801-364-1581	www.avalanche.org/~uac
Tri-Canyon area (Alta)	801-742-0830	www.avalanche.org/~uac
Mount Ogden and south	801-626-8600	www.avalanche.org/~uac
North Wasatch Mountains, Bear River (Logan)	435-797-4146	www.avalanche.org/~vac/braic
La Sal Mountains (Moab)	435-259-7669	www.avalanche.org/~lsafc
Statewide Snowmobile Hotline	800-648-7433	

Washington

Washington's Cascade Range, Olympic Mountains (Seattle)	206-526-6677	www.nwaa.noaa.gov

Wyoming

Teton and Wind River mountains (Jackson)	307-733-2664	www.jhavalanche.org

: Avalanche Forecasts Canada

> **Avalanche Forecasts Canada**   www.avalanche.ca

Alberta

Waterton Lakes National Park	www.avalanche.ca/weather/bulletins
Kananaskis	www.avalanche.ca/weather/bulletins

Alberta/British Columbia

Canadian Rockies	403-243-7253	www.avalanche.ca/weather/bulletins

British Columbia

Western Canada (Columbia Mountains, Rockies, south coast of B.C.)	800-667-1105	www.avalanche.ca/weather/bulletins
Banff, Kootenay and Yoho national parks	403-762-1460	www.avalanche.ca/weather/bulletins
Glacier National Park (Roger Pass)	250-814-5232	www.avalanche.ca/weather/bulletins
Jasper National Park	780-852-6176	www.avalanche.ca/weather/bulletins

: Avalanche Forecasts Europe

> **Map of the European Alps**

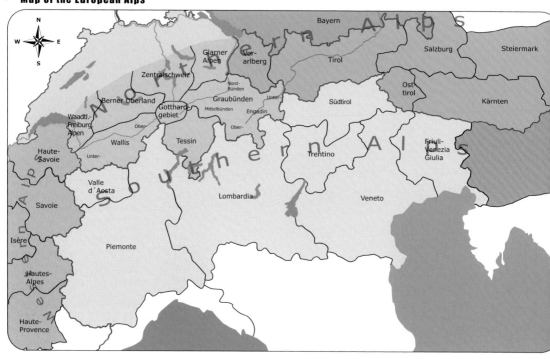

Switzerland

Deutsch	+41 848800 187	www.slf.ch
Français	+41 848800 187	www.slf.ch
Italiano	+41 848800 187	www.slf.ch

Germany

Bayern	+49(0)89 9214 1210	www.lawinenwarndienst.bayern.de

Austria

Vorarlberg	+43(0)5522 1588	www.lawine.at
Salzburg	+43(0)662 1588	www.lawine.at
Tirol	+43(0)512 1588	www.lawine.at
Steiermark	+43(0)316 1588	www.lawine.at
Kärnten	+43(0)463 1588	www.lawine.at

Italy

Valle d´Aosta	+390165 776300	
Piemonte	+39011 3185555	www.regione.piemonte.it/meteo/neve.htm
Trentino		www.provincia.tn.it/meteo
Veneto	+390436 79221	www.arpa.veneto.it
Südtirol	+390471 271177	www.provincia.bz.it
Friuli-Venezia G.		www.regionefvg.it/bolniv/bolniv.htm

France
+33 (0) 892-681020

Haute-Savoie	choice: *74	www.meteo.fr/temps/france/avalanches/
Savoie	choice: *73	www.meteo.fr/temps/france/avalanches/
Isère	choice: *38	www.meteo.fr/temps/france/avalanches/
Hautes-Alpes	choice: *05	www.meteo.fr/temps/france/avalanches/
Haute-Provence	choice: *04	www.meteo.fr/temps/france/avalanches/

European Avalanche Danger Rating

1(low): The snowpack is generally well bonded and stable. Triggering is possible only with high additional loads[2] on a few very steep extreme slopes.[4] Only a few small natural[6] avalanches (sluffs) possible. No hazard from avalanches. Virtually no restrictions on off-piste & backcountry skiing & travel.

2(moderate): The snowpack is moderately well bonded on some[1] steep[3] slopes, otherwise generally well bonded. Triggering is possible with high additional loads,[2] particularly on the steep[3] slopes indicated in the bulletin. Large natural[6] avalanches not likely. Virtually no hazard from natural avalanches. Generally favourable conditions. Routes should still be selected with care, especially on steep[3] slopes of the aspect[5] and altitude indicated.

3(considerable): The snowpack is moderately to weakly bonded on many[1] steep[3] slopes. Triggering is possible, sometimes even with low additional loads.[2] The bulletin may indicate many slopes which are particularly affected. In certain conditions, medium and occasionally large sized natural[6] avalanches may occur. Traffic and individual buildings in hazardous areas are at risk in certain cases. Precautions should be taken in these areas. Off-piste and backcountry skiing and travel should only be carried out by experienced persons able to evaluate avalanche hazard. Steep[3] slopes of the aspect[5] and altitude indicated should be avoided.

4(high): The snowpack is weakly bonded in most[1] places. Triggering is probable even with low additional loads[2] on many steep[3] slopes. In some conditions, frequent medium or large sized natural[6] avalanches are likely. Avalanches may be of large magnitude. In hazardous areas, closure of road and other transport is recommended in some circumstances. Off-piste and backcountry skiing and travel should be restricted to low-angled slopes; areas at the bottom of slopes may also be hazardous.

5(very high): The snowpack is generally weakly bonded and largely unstable. Numerous large natural[6] avalanches are likely, even on moderately steep terrain. Extensive safety measures (closures and evacuation) are necessary. No off-piste or backcountry skiing or travel should be undertaken.

> Notes

[1] Generally described in more detail in the avalanche bulletin (e.g., altitude, slope aspect, type of terrain, etc.).

[2] Additional load: high — e.g., group of skiers, pistemachine, avalanche blasting. Low — e.g., skier, walker.

[3] Steep slopes: slopes with an incline of more than 30° degrees.

[4] Steep extreme slopes: those which are particularly unfavourable in terms of the incline, terrain profile, proximity to ridge, smoothness of underlying ground surface.

[5] Aspect: compass bearing directly down the slope.

[6] Natural: Without human assistance.

Canadian Avalanche Danger Rating

Danger Level and Color	Probability and Trigger	Recommended Action
Low	Natural avalanches very unlikely. Human triggered avalanches unlikely.	Travel is generally safe. Normal caution advised.
Moderate	Natural avalanches unlikely. Human triggered avalanches possible.	Use caution in steeper terrain on certain aspects.
Considerable	Natural avalanches possible. Human triggered avalanches probable.	Be increasingly cautious in steeper terrain.
High	Natural and human triggered avalanches likely.	Travel in avalanche terrain is not recommended.
Extreme	Widespread natural or human triggered avalanches certain.	Travel in avalanche terrain should be avoided and confined to low angle terrain, well away from avalanche path runouts.

Avalanche Education

USA

American Avalanche Association	970-946-0822	www.americanavalancheassociation.org
American Mountain Guides Association	303-271-0984	www.amga.com
CyberSpace Avalanche Center		www.csac.org

USA and Canada

avalanche.org	www.avalanche.org/~education

Canada

Canadian Avalanche Association	250-837-2435	www.avalanche.ca/rac
Association of Canadian Mountain Guides	403-678-2885	www.acmg.ca

Weather Forecasts

USA

National Weather Service	www.nws.noaa.gov

Canada

Environment Canada	www.weatheroffice.ec.gc.ca

☞Thorsten Indra

Country and Area Infos
USA/Canada
maps and air photos

www.topozone.com
www.usgs.gov

Rescue
Mountain Rescue Association

www.mra.org

> In case of an accident always dial 911. If friends are overdue, call the local sheriff or police department.

Wilderness Medical and Rescue

USA

National Ski Patrol	www.nsp.org

Canada

Sirius Wilderness Medicine	www.siriusmed.com
Canadian Ski Patrol System	www.csps.ca

: Avalanche Hazard Evaluation Training

Alaska

Alaska Avalanche School, Mountain Safety Center   907-3453566
9140 Brewsters Dr.
Anchorage, AK 99516

Wyoming

American Avalanche Institute, Inc.   307-733-3315
P.O. Box 308
Wilson, WY 83014

Canada

Back Country Avalanche Institute Alberta   403-678-4102
P.O. Box 1050
Canmore, Alberta T0L 0M0, Canada

Canadian Avalanche Association Trainings School   604-837-2435
P.O. Box 2759
Revelstoke, B.C. V0E 2S0, Canada

Washington

Northwest Avalanche Institute   206-663-2597
Crystal Mountain Blvd.
Crystal Mountain, WA 98022

Colorado

National Skipatrol System, Inc.   303-988-1111
133 S. Van Gordon St. Suite 100
Lakewood, CO 80228

Avalanche and Freeride/Freeski Camps in Europe

Mountain Surf Club   +41-(0)33-823 2724
(German, French and English spoken)
Post Box 109
CH-3800 Interlaken, Switzerland
Internet: www.mountainsurfclub.com

> > Before signing up for a course, try to get an idea of the instructors' background. We recommend this because there is no legal requirement for instructor qualifications. In general, **Association of Canadian Mountain Guides (ACMG)** or **American Mountain Guides Association (AMGA)** and internationally certified mountain guides are a good bet. **Professional members** of the **American Avalanche Association** or the **Canadian Avalanche Association** are also experienced avalanche people. Beware of riding or skiing enthusiasts who don't have much more knowledge and experience than you do. Anybody is allowed to offer courses!

> > Information on anything related to powder and freeriding / freeskiing
> > WWW. **POWDERGUIDE** .com

: Emergency Calls
No charge calls

USA	911
Canada	911
Europe	112

Alpine Emergencies – SAR

Germany	19222
Switzerland	1414
Austria	140
Italy / South Tyrol	118

Sastrugi stand up to the wind

⊡Tyrolean Avalanche Warning Service

: Bibliography

We would like to thank the authors and publishers of the following books and publications for their expertise and suggestions (selected reference):

The English ones ...

> Daffern, Tony. **Avalanche Safety for Skiers, Climbers and Snowboarders.**
> (Calgary, Rocky Mountain Books, 1993)
> Fredston, Jill and Doug, Fesler. **Snow Sense.**
> (Anchorage, Alaska: Alaska Mountain Safety Center, 1994)
> Jamieson, Bruce and Torsten Geldsetzer. **Avalanche Accidents in Canada, Vol. 4.**
> (Revelstoke, British Columbia: Canadian Avalanche Association, 1996)
> Jamieson, Bruce, and Jennie McDonald. **Free Riding in Avalanche Terrain.**
> (Calgary, Alberta: Canadian Avalanche Association, 1999)
> McClung, David, and Peter Schaerer. **The Avalanche Handbook.**
> (Seattle, Washington: The Mountaineers, 1993)
> Tremper, Bruce. **Staying Alive in Avalanche Terrain.**
> (Seattle, Washington: The Mountaineers, 2001)

Published in German

> Munter, Werner. **3x3 Lawinen**, Hrsg. Agentur Pohl und Schellhammer,
> 2. Aufl. Garmisch-Partenkirchen 1999
> Geyer, Peter / Pohl, Wolfgang. **Skibergsteigen/Variantenfahren** Alpinlehrplan Band 4,
> BLV Verlagsgesellschaft, München 1998
> Österreichisches Autorenteam, **Lawinenhandbuch**, Hrsg. Land Tirol /
> Verlagsanstalt Tyrolia, 7. Aufl. Innsbruck 2000
> Bericht zur Tagung 10.-14.01.1994, **Lawinen und Rechtsfragen**, SLF / Davos
> Seminarbericht 25.-28.01.2000, **Winteralpinismus – Rechtsfragen**, Kühtai / Tirol
> Engler, Martin / Mersch, Jan. **Die weiße Gefahr: Schnee und Lawinen**;
> Erfahrungen / Mechanismen / Risikomanagement, Verlag Engler, Sulzberg 2001
> Oster, Peter. **Erste Hilfe Outdoor**, Ziel Verlag, Berlin 2003
> Dörner, Dietrich. **Die Logik des Misslingens. Strategisches Denken in komplexen Situationen**,
> Rowohlt Verlag, Hamburg 1989
> Hoffman, Michael. **Lawinengefahr**, BLV Verlagsgesellschaft, München 2000

: About the Authors :

Tobias Kurzeder

Born in 1974

Freerider since 1993

Snowboard and mountain bike trips and expeditions

Snowboard instructor, guide and outdoor trainer

Numerous publications on freeriding, risk management and avalanches

Studies geography and politics

Lives in Freiburg, Germany

Holger Feist

Born in 1970

Freerider since 1987

World Cup competitor for many years

Engineer

Snowboard instructor and guide

Product manager and R&D specialist in the snowboard industry

Numerous expeditions with snowboards and mountain bikes in Kamtchatka, Tibet, Lebanon...

Lives in Munich, Germany

Patrick Reimann

Born in 1968

Freerider since 1994

Freeride instructor and manager at Mountain Surf Club

Launched freeride and avalanche camps for snowboarders in 1995

Co-author of a guidebook to the Eastern Bernese Alps

Loves soul riding wide and steep slopes

Wants to get old as a freerider

Lives in Interlaken, Switzerland

Peter Oster

Born in 1972

Paramedic, Wilderness-EMT

Developed first-aid courses for outdoor sports

Numerous epic solo tours in Canada and Lapland

Master's degree in geography and biology (M.SC)

Lives in Freiburg, Germany

Many thanks to ...
All of those who contributed to this book.

Thanks to ...
Alan Stark, Ibo Kilicoglu, Werner Munter, Stefan Österreicher, Christoph Ditzfelbinger, Dale Atkins, Jan Imberi, Karin Betzler, Holger Peller, Judith Wagner, Mark Mueller, Knox Williams, Reid Banson, Karen Righthand, Bill Grout
...for their cooperation.

Thanks to ...
Richard Walch, Thorsten Indra, Patrick Nairz, Rudi Mair, Raimund Mayr, Andi Schwarz, Bernd Zenke, Basti Pölzelbauer, Martin Engler, André Roth, Baschi Bender, Stefan Hunziker, Stefan Schütz, Jancsi Hadic, Reiner Pickl, Ralf Hochhauser, Jeff Curtes, John Speer, Tobias Hafele, Dan Ferrer, Helmut Mittermayr
... for the photos.

We would also like to give our thanks to the following institutions:

Tyrolean Avalanche Warning Service

Bavarian Avalanche Warning Service

Swiss Federal Institute for Snow and Avalanche Research, FISAR, Davos

Colorado Avalanche Information Center

Thanks to ...
Christoph Ditzfelbinger, Werner Munter, Dale Atkins, Patrick Nairz, Bruce Tremper
... for corrections and constructive criticism.

Special Thanks to
Daniel Emerson, Alan Stark, Stefan Österreicher

And last but not least thanks to our sponsors / partners:

: Glossary

airblast
An air pressure wave that runs beyond the visible avalanche front or deposited snow.

analog transceiver
An avalanche beacon that emits an acoustic signal that grows louder the closer it gets to a beacon worn by an avalanche victim.

aspect
The compass direction of a slope opposite its fall line. Also called slope orientation.

avalanche beacon
A radio worn by freeriders and freeskiers and used to locate people who are buried in an avalanche. Also called avalanche transceiver.

avalanche path
The entire area in which an avalanche moves.

chinook, see foehn

cohesion
The degree of stickiness that a snowpack possesses. Once a failure has taken place, cohesive snow will result in slab avalanches, non-cohesive snow will result in loose-snow avalanches.

cornice
An overhanging buildup of snow caused by wind on the lee side of ridges. Cornices sometimes overhang the lee side of a slope with many tons of snow.

corn snow
This type of snow is composed of large granular crystals formed in repeated cycles of melting and refreezing, often days, weeks or months after it has fallen to the ground. Corn snow is also known as spring snow.

creep
An internal deformation of the snowpack reflecting the snow's ability to flow like a very dense liquid.

critical amount of new snow
An expression introduced by Werner Munter to denote the amount of new snow that creates dangerous conditions for freeriding. When the critical amount of new snow is reached, the avalanche danger is Considerable or higher.

concave
A bowl-like shape of a slope or plain. The snowpack in concave slopes is subject to compression stresses in the flatter sections at the foot of the slope.

convex
An outwardly curved slope shape characterized by tensile stresses in the slope's upper section, where the snowpack is pulled down by gravity.

cornice
An overhang of snow formed by wind action over the leeward (downwind) and/or the steeper side of a ridge.

cross loading
Deposition of wind-driven snow across slopes as opposed to down slopes. May fill up gullies with windblown snow.

crown or fracture line
This term refers to the top fracture line of a slab avalanche.

crust
A layer of hard snow lying upon a soft layer.

cup crystal
A hollow, cup-shaped crystal created by faceting. Depth hoar consists of cup crystals.

deposition zone
The area where the bulk of the snow carried down in an avalanche comes to rest.

depth hoar or sugar snow
Recrystallized snow found particularly often in the bottom layers of shallow snowpacks

after periods of low surface temperatures. Depth hoar forms in a process of metamorphosis called faceting. This type of snow often forms dangerous gliding layers for snow slabs.

digital transceivers
Digital transceivers are equipped with two antennas and a digital display that shows the direction and distance to the buried person.

direct-action avalanche
Direct-action avalanches are avalanches that release during or shortly after a storm.

faceting
Crystal growth by the deposition of ice on snow grains caused by water vapor rising through the snowpack. This process is responsible for the formation of depth hoar.

firn snow
Snow that did not thaw the previous summer(s) and is therefore more than one year old.

foehn
A relatively warm and strong wind. A Foehn is caused when cloud buildup at the windward side of a mountain range causes precipitation. Moist air is lifted, loses its moisture in the form of precipitation and cools down very little (approx. 0.5°C/100meters). As it descends on the lee side, it is warmed by compression (approx. 1°C/100meter). This often results in warm and windy conditions and thawing of the snowpack on the lee side. **ground avalanche**
Wet-snow avalanches that release in spring and pick up masses of rock or soil along with the entire snowpack right down to the ground surface (soil, rock, grass, etc.). Also called a full-depth avalanche.

human trigger
Avalanche release caused by humans, whether intentionally or unintentionally.

Loose-snow avalanche or point release
Loose-snow avalanches originate in cohesionless snow and start from a point, gathering more and more snow as they descend.

melt-freeze crust
A layer of snow that has been warmed until liquid water forms between grains and then freezes to form a relatively strong layer.

melt-freeze metamorphism
As soon as snow has reached a temperature of 32°F (0°C), it can contain liquid water. This liquid water leads to grains becoming larger. If the snow temperature drops below freezing again, the water freezes.

natural avalanche or natural release
Any avalanche that occurs without being triggered by active avalanche-control procedures or without accidental triggering by a snow traveler.

powder avalanche
Powder avalanches are an aerosol of fine, diffused snow that behaves as a sharply bounded body of dense gas.

remote triggering
The release of an avalanche in an area far away from the spot where the stress has been applied to the snowpack.

rime
A deposit of ice formed by supercooled water droplets that freeze upon contact with a cold surface. Rime can accumulate on the windward side of rocks, trees or structures, or on falling crystals of snow.

ripples/dunes
Wave-like patterns on the snow surface caused by wind, which leads to dangerous wind-blown snow accumulation. Ripples point in a downwind direction.

rounding
Within the snowpack, the process of rounding turns star-shaped hexagonal snowflakes into smaller, more-rounded grains that bond together.

rotten snow, or slush
Water-saturated snow that has lost its original cohesion by intense thawing.
runout zone
The runout zone is the portion of the avalanche path where snow slows down and comes to rest.
rutschblock test
A test used to determine the stability of the snowpack in a given spot. For a long time it was thought that spot testing could help determine the overall stability of a slope. Unfortunately this was an error that caused many accidents. The information gathered from a great number of such shear tests can be helpful for assessing the hazard level in a given area. In practical courses, rutschblock tests should only be used to demonstrate how avalanches form.
sastrugi
Erosion ridges on the snow surface caused by wind. Sastrugi point into the wind.
settlement
Densification and strengthening of the snowpack under the action of gravity and rounding.
shear strength
The force that opposes shear stress, also known as static friction. Shear strength determines the stability of a given slope.
shear stress
The force that moves a layer of snow deposited on top of another layer. If shear stress exceeds static friction of a layer of cohesive snow, it begins to slide and forms a slab avalanche.
sintering
The joining together of ice grains by the formation of necks between adjacent grains. See rounding.
slab
A slab is an area of cohesive snow. Slabs fracture when the load of snow over a weak layer exceeds the shear strength of that layer. Slab is often used incorrectly as a synonym or short form for slab avalanche.
slab avalanche
A type of avalanche that starts when an area of cohesive snow begins to slide on a weak layer within the snowpack or on smooth ground. Slab avalanches have a usually well-defined fracture line at the point where the slab broke away from the rest of the snowpack.
snow sluff
A small snow slide usually made up of loose snow.
spring snow, see corn snow
surface hoar
Crystals shaped like feathers or needles that grow upward from the snow surface. Surface hoar grows most often in calm, relatively clear nights at low temperatures. When buried by later snowfalls, it can be a persistent weak layer.
temperature gradient
The temperature gradient is the difference in temperature between different layers of the snowpack. Large temperature gradients favor the formation of depth hoar.
terrain trap
A gully, depression, bowl, V-shaped channel or other terrain feature that increases the chance of getting caught in an avalanche.
whumpfing
The sound of collapsing layers of snow and fractures propagating within the snowpack. Whumpfing noises are alarm signals.
Wind loading
Deposition of additional snow by the wind that increases avalanche danger.

Red Bull / Miles Holden △ New Zealand ⚐ Eriksson Johan

: Index

Korjaksi, 11,338 feet (3,456 meters), a volcano in △ Kamtchatka, Russia. ⊕ Bernhard Spöttel